W9-AFC-097

the art of metal clay

REVISED AND EXPANDED EDITION

the art of metal clay

REVISED AND EXPANDED EDITION

Techniques for Creating Jewelry
and Decorative Objects

SHERRI HAAB

WATSON-GUPTILL PUBLICATIONS
New York

3D metal clay charms by Lisa Call.
Photo by the artist.

Copyright © 2010 by Sherri Haab.
All rights reserved.
Published in the United States in 2010
by Watson-Guptill Publications,
an imprint of the Crown Publishing Group,
a division of Random House, Inc., New York

www.crownpublishing.com
www.watsonguptill.com

WATSON-GUPTILL is a registered trademark and
the WG and Horse designs are registered trade-
marks of Random House, Inc.

Designed by Kara Plikaitis

Library of Congress Cataloging-in-Publication
Data

Haab, Sherri.
 The art of metal clay : techniques for creating
jewelry and decorative objects / Sherri Haab. —
Rev. and expanded.
   p. cm.
 Includes index.
 ISBN 978-0-8230-9932-0
1. Metal-work. 2. Jewelry making. 3. Precious
metal clay. I. Title.
 TT213.H33 2009
 739.27—dc22
            2009043781

Printed in China

First printing, 2010
1 2 3 4 5 6 7 8 / 17 16 15 14 13 12 11 10

dedication & acknowledgments

To my sweet family, Dan, Rachel, Michelle, and David.
You bring so much joy to my life!

Many thanks to the artists who contributed projects and photos for this book, and for members of the PMC guild including Tim McCreight for technical help and encouragement. A big thank you to Jackie Truty, Speedy Peacock, Mardel Rein, Kevin Whitmore, and Anthony Squillacci, Jr. My gratitude to my editor Joy Aquilino and the staff at Watson-Guptill for all of the hard work and dedication they put into publishing beautiful books.

Contents

Nouveau Diamond Necklace #3 by Shahasp Valentine. Rhodolite garnets and diamonds set in PMC3 and fired in place, with pearls and sterling silver. Photo by the artist.

Introduction

When *The Art of Metal Clay* was first released in 2003, there were only a few books available about this fascinating new material. Since then the popularity of this craft can only be described as phenomenal. Being so easy to use and requiring only a few simple tools, it's no wonder that metal clay has captured the attention of jewelry artists and casual hobbyists alike. Many early enthusiasts quickly embraced this new material and started metal clay cottage industries, from selling finished pieces on the popular website Etsy.com to providing retail supplies and tools. Nowadays, metal clay has found its way into community education programs, guilds, regional workshops, bead shows, and even formal college credit courses!

Although powder metallurgy is nothing new, the use of metal in this form as a craft material is unique and is still evolving with the development of new clay formulations and techniques. If you're unfamiliar with metal clay, a simple explanation will help you to understand what it is: Metal clay simply consists of microscopic metal particles suspended in a mix of an organic binder and water. Metal clay looks very much like modeling clay. It's smooth and pliable, and can be worked with your hands. According to metal clay manufacturers it is nontoxic and safe to use. It can be textured, rolled, carved, or sculpted to make jewelry, beads, vessels, and small sculptures. Once a metal clay object is fired, the binder burns away and the metal particles sinter, or fuse, together. The final product emerges as a metal piece that can be marked as such. Metal clay is available in fine silver (.999), gold (22K), and, more recently, bronze (89% copper, 11% tin) and copper. After firing the clay it can be finished using traditional metalworking techniques. The finished metal pieces can then be utilized to incorporate techniques such as enameling and etching, or used in combination with other materials such as glass, polymer clay, or resin to create mixed-media pieces.

What is exciting about metal clay is that you don't need to be an experienced metalsmith to make beautifully finished metal objects. As mentioned earlier, this quality has contributed greatly to the popularity of metal clay. If you already work with metal, metal clay can inspire new ideas and add dimension to your work. It provides new techniques and ways of forming metal that will change the way you think about it—the possibilities are endless. For beginners or crafters who haven't worked with metal before, it's a way to create metal objects without having to go through the steps that traditional metalwork usually requires. Aside from being a shortcut to creating metal objects, metal clay has its own unique properties. Artists are drawn to its versatility as a medium, and many are content to work with metal clay exclusively, developing jewelry and gallery pieces that are able to stand on their own.

The projects in this book were designed to allow you to explore different techniques with various types of metal clay in addition to being used as inspirations for your own designs. Each project suggests a type of metal clay that has specific properties that work well for a particular technique. You may find you prefer one clay type to another. As you begin to understand the properties of each type of clay, it's easy to make substitutions. One final note: Be sure to follow the manufacturer's firing instructions for the type of clay you're using.

part 1

Metal Clay Essentials

Types of Metal Clay

Metal clay is available in many different formulas. Manufacturers originally offered only fine silver or gold with low-fire versions of both. More recently, bronze and copper clays have been developed and introduced to the market. Prices for precious metals have dramatically increased, making bronze and copper an affordable alternative for those who have avoided metal clay due to its expense. In addition to being affordable, bronze and copper possess unique qualities such as strength as well as options for color and patina.

Manufacturers and retailers of metal clay also offer accessories and products to accompany the clay. Products from different brands of metal clay currently on the market can be used together in the same piece. Keep in mind, though, that the shrinkage rates and firing temperatures need to be compatible when firing different clay types together. In addition, bronze and copper require specific tools, supplies, and firing conditions.

SILVER AND GOLD CLAY PRODUCTS

Precious Metal Clay® (PMC®) was developed in Japan in 1991 by Mitsubishi Materials Corporation. In 1996, PMC was introduced to the United States. Silver and gold metal clays were the first to be developed, followed by PMC+, PMC paste, PMC slip, PMC paper, and then PMC3. Mitsubishi continues to produce new PMC products. PMC is available both online and from certain jewelry-making suppliers.

Art Clay™ products are manufactured by Aida Chemical Industries, a company that recycles metals. In 1991, Aida Research and Development obtained the patent for the manufacturing process for the metal clays now known as Art Clay Silver and Art Clay Gold. Art Clay Silver is available from various retail outlets specializing in jewelry-making supplies and online.

Both PMC and Art Clay offer extensive educational programs. The PMC Guild offers a newsletter, conferences, workshops, and certification programs. Art Clay Silver also offers workshops and certification programs. They continue to develop and improve their metal clays and products.

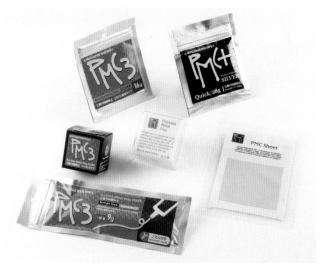

PMC products come in different formulas, including PMC, PMC3, PMC+, PMC Syringe, and PMC Sheet.

PMC Products

Each PMC product has distinctive qualities. A particular project or technique, or even your artistic style, may dictate which clay to use. Whether sculpting, molding, texturing, or incorporating stones, different clays have properties that make one preferable to another.

PMC Standard (or "Original PMC") was the first metal clay developed. Precious Metal Clay Standard consists of flake-shaped silver particles with more binder in between the particles, making it a smooth clay with excellent workability. This clay shrinks twenty-five to thirty percent during the firing process—more than any of the other formulas, because it contains more binder—so it's great to use for small projects, including charms and finely detailed pieces. It's also more porous and less dense in its finished state than other types of metal clay, and therefore isn't as strong. For this reason, PMC Standard isn't recommended for rings, clasps, or other pieces that will endure a lot of stress.

PMC+ is a great all-purpose choice for most projects. Its silver particles are denser than PMC Standard, making it a bit stiffer to work with. However, the end result after firing is a stronger product. Because it is denser than PMC Standard, it shrinks less. This type of clay can be fired at several different temperatures and for shorter lengths of time than PMC Standard, which gives you the advantage of being able to fire the clay with cork, glass, and certain stones—all of which require lower temperatures.

PMC3 is a versatile, low-fire silver clay. It has smaller, more refined particles and less binder than PMC Standard and PMC+. This makes it strong and dense, with less shrinkage than other PMC types. The particle shapes and density of PMC3 allow it to be fired as low as 1110°F (599°C) as well as for short periods of time. The short firing periods allow for the clay to be torch-fired with an inexpensive portable handheld butane torch, while low temperatures allow certain stones and glass to be fired with the clay. This is exciting for those who want to try metal clay but do not want to invest in a kiln right away.

PMC Paste (Slip) is premixed paste, or slip, with a glue consistency that you can use to "glue" or attach PMC pieces together, fill in joins, or create textures on the surface of a piece. This formula is available in both PMC+ and PMC3 formulas.

PMC Syringe is like thick slip in a ready-to-use syringe. You can use syringe clay to make strong attachments to adhere elements to each other, to fill in grooves or cracks, or to create a "line" or rope of clay as a decorative element. After opening, keep the uncapped syringe submerged in water. It is available in both PMC+ and PMC3 formulas.

PMC+ Sheet and Long Sheet are paper-thin sheets of clay. They stay flexible and do not dry out while you are working with them. You can fold them, cut them with scissors, punch them out with a hole-puncher, or weave or braid thin strips. Layers of Sheet can be laminated to make thicker sheets of clay, and Long Sheet gives you extra length when needed for a project.

Pure Metals & Alloys

The numbers associated with silver and gold indicate the purity of the metal. Fine silver is considered pure at .999 millesimal fineness. With 24 out of 24 parts being gold, 24K gold is considered pure. In comparison to fine silver, sterling silver consists of 92.5% silver and 7.5% copper, while 14K gold consists of 58.5% gold and other metals, such as copper and silver.

Fine silver and gold are softer than alloys such as sterling silver, and therefore consideration should be given in designing metal clay jewelry that requires strength, such as rings.

Space Flower 2 by Nancy Hamilton. This centerpiece was made with PMC+, sterling silver chain, and pearls. Photo by the artist.

PMC 22K Gold Because PMC 22K Gold clay is an alloy of 91.7% gold and 8.3% silver, it has a rich yellow color. This clay fires at similar temperatures to other formulas of PMC, which allows you to layer or fire it with silver clay. PMC 22K Gold has replaced the original 24K Gold version that used to require firing at a higher temperature. It also shrinks less than the previous version.

Aura 22 is a thin, gold "slip." It can be painted on fired silver metal clay or sterling silver, providing a rich gold layer to the surface. The slip is then refired onto the surface.

Art Clay Silver

Art Clay Silver is similar to PMC metal clay in that both companies offer silver and gold metal clay products. PMC and Art Clay vary in texture and drying times due to their proprietary blends of moisture content and binder, which is unique in each brand. Art Clay offers many choices for specific projects, as well as accompanying products and tools that are very useful with metal clay. All of the Art Clay Silver clays, which are dense (and therefore very strong), can be fired at low temperatures or with a torch.

Art Clay Silver Basic is an all-purpose silver metal clay that can be fired at several temperatures, including low firing temperatures that allow it to be used in conjunction with glass, cork clay, and certain stones.

Art Clay Silver Slow-Dry contains a different binder than Art Clay Silver Basic. This feature allows the clay to dry slowly, providing the artist with more working time. It is recommended for those who live in dry climates where clay usually dries too quickly due to the lack of humidity. Slow-Dry must be thoroughly dry before firing. It is perfect for projects such as rings, braids, or fine ropes. Scraps of this clay should not be mixed with other types of clay.

Art Clay Silver 650/1200 Low-Fire is the lowest firing clay of the Art Clay Silver types. It can be fired at low enough temperatures to embed sterling silver findings. It can also be fired with dichroic glass cabochons and ceramics. In addition, some natural stones can be fired into the clay without being destroyed in the firing process.

Art Clay Silver 650/1200 Low-Fire Slow-Dry can be fired at the same low temperatures as 650/1200 Low-Fire, but dries slower, like Slow-Dry. It's great for making rings or other projects where a longer working time is desirable.

Art Clay Silver 650/1200 Low-Fire Paste can be used to attach pieces of unfired clay, to fill in cracks, or to create textures. This product can be used when slip is required for a project and can be painted over leaves, pods, or other organic matter and then fired.

Art Clay Silver Overlay Paste is specially formulated for use on glazed porcelain or ceramics. Thin layers can be painted onto glass, porcelain, or ceramic as decorative painted elements, and fired. The paste can also be used like slip to attach unfired pieces together.

Art Clay Silver 650/1200 Low-Fire Syringe is a soft formula that is prepackaged in a ready-to-use syringe. You can use it to make fine lines of clay, surround stones, or fill cracks.

Art Clay Silver Oil Paste is formulated to stick to metal. Use it to attach previously fired pieces, to make repairs, or to fill cracks. Fire Oil Paste at 1472°F (800°C) when refiring pieces repaired with it.

Art Clay Silver Paper Type is thin and flexible. It can be cut, punched, or folded. Paper Type can be layered to make thicker sheets.

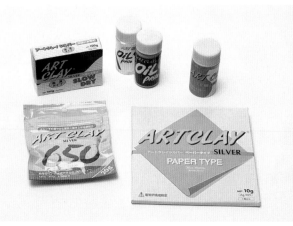

Art Clay Silver offers a variety of silver and gold clay products. Shown are the Slow-Dry, Oil Paste, Paste, Paper Type, and 650/1200.

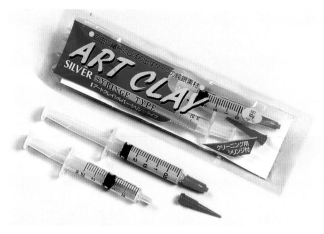

Art Clay Silver products include Syringe Type, a soft formula that is prepackaged in a ready-to-use syringe.

Art Clay Gold Use Art Clay Gold as you would any silver metal clay. Art Clay Gold fires at a higher temperature than silver, 1813°F (989°C) for 60 minutes. After firing, the gold is 22K.

Art Clay Gold Paste is a liquid formula of gold that can be applied to silver or painted onto glass or porcelain. It comes with a medium that can be used to thin the product down to a glaze consistency.

BRONZE AND COPPER CLAY PRODUCTS

The first versions of bronze and copper clays were developed by chemist Bill Struve. Bill's BRONZclay™ was introduced in 2008, followed by COPPRclay™ in 2009. Recycled copper is used to make bronze and copper clays and both types are distributed by Rio Grande.

Hadar Jacobson, an early pioneer in the development of bronze and copper clays, has her own line of metal clays. Hadar's Clay™ is available in copper and bronze powder formulas, and can be mixed by simply adding water as needed to make the clay. She also has quick-fire versions, which do not require carbon for sintering. The advantage to Hadar's dry powder formulations is that you do not have to worry about shelf life.

Art Clay has a brand of copper clay. Art Clay Copper™ clay is a special formulation that can be fired without carbon. The clay sinters in the presence of oxygen but requires quenching and then pickling to remove oxidation.

BRONZclay

BRONZclay consists of 11% tin, 89% copper, water, and a nontoxic binder. The binding materials vaporize completely during the kiln-firing process, leaving a solid bronze piece with a density that is ninety percent as dense as cast bronze. Bronze clay must be layered in carbon and in a closed container when fired to reduce its exposure to oxygen. It can be fired with copper and silver clays under certain conditions (see page 35).

COPPRclay

COPPRclay consists of pure copper, water, and a nontoxic binder. The binding materials vaporize completely during the kiln-firing process, leaving a solid copper piece with a density of more than 95% cast copper. Like bronze clay, copper clay must be layered in carbon and in a closed container when fired to reduce oxygen. Copper clay can also be fired with silver and bronze clays.

Hadar's Clay-Copper

Hadar's Clay-Copper is a powdered form of copper and binder to which water is added to make the clay. Hadar's copper is also available in a quick-fire version. Her website includes instructions for various firing methods, including open-shelf firing methods that do not require carbon.

Art Clay Copper

Art Clay Copper does not require a reduced oxygen environment to sinter properly, meaning it can be fired on a kiln shelf rather than being buried in carbon. To remove oxidation after firing, the piece is quickly quenched and then pickled.

ACCENT SILVER

Accent Silver is a silver slip that can be fired over other metals to provide a silver-plated finish. It can be fired over prefired or cast brass, bronze, or copper metals. The metal to be coated must be clean prior to applying Accent Silver. The piece must then also be fired in carbon to prevent oxidation and to promote proper sintering. Cool Tools has an excellent video tutorial for more information on how to use the product.

Accent Silver allows you to add a silver finish.

Cuff bracelets by Mardel Rein using BRONZclay, COPPRclay, and Accent Silver. Heat and liver of sulfur were used to patina the surface. Photo by Bill Lemke.

Tools & Supplies

Making jewelry with metal clay requires very little space and just a few simple tools. You can set up a working area at your kitchen table or in a small studio space. Keep the area neat and clean as you work, and your tools and supplies close at hand. The best part about using metal clay is that the tools are easy to obtain from craft or jewelry-making suppliers. You might already own many of the necessary items, as they are commonly used for polymer clay and other crafts. You may also be able to substitute tools you already have for some of the following suggested tools.

If you already use silver or gold metal clay, many of the tools you're familiar with can be used interchangeably for bronze and copper clays. However, a few tools are especially good for texturing bronze and copper, which are heavier-bodied clays than silver or gold. I mention a few tools that make working with these clays easier in the following list; you may want to add these to your tool kit.

Unless your silver metal clay tools can be washed between uses, it's a good idea to keep them separate from your bronze and copper clay tools. Silver will attempt to alloy with other metals if bits are embedded in the unfired pieces. In my experience, texture sheets that had silver clay residue had no adverse affects on copper clay; however, coating silver clay with bronze slip proved to be disastrous. When in doubt, keep the two sets of tools clean and separate. Supplies such as sanding papers and files are inexpensive and disposable, making it easy to designate a set for each specific type of clay you're using.

BASIC METAL CLAY SUPPLIES

The supply list for each project in this book includes "basic metal clay tools." These are the common items, described here, that are needed for working with metal clay. I keep them together in a tool kit so that they are readily available for my project at hand. This way, I need only to gather the specialty or extra items required for a specific project, and then I'm ready to get started. The basic tools and supplies needed include many common household items such as olive oil, playing cards, and a spray bottle, as well as a few simple craft and ceramic tools. Look around and add your own favorites to this basic list.

Work Surface

Plastic mats, laminate countertop surfaces, or Teflon sheets are good surfaces to use while forming metal clay. Don't panic if the clay sticks to the work surface. Leave the clay item in place, and as it dries it will release from the surface. I prefer working on a thin sheet of Teflon because I can peel the Teflon from the back of the wet clay piece and easily move it to a warming device. Certain metal surfaces, such as aluminum, react with metal clay, causing the finished pieces to warp and discolor. Do not place metal clay on aluminum foil or aluminum cookie sheets. In general, avoid tools with aluminum as well, although minimal contact with aluminum such as cutting shapes with cookie cutters may not affect the silver.

Olive Oil or Badger Balm

Keep a small dish of olive oil or a solid ointment called Badger Balm® close at hand. Apply a thin film of oil or balm to your hands, tools, and work surface to keep the clay from sticking and drying out. Reapply oil as the clay starts to collect on your fingers. Olive oil or Badger Balm can also be used as a mold release. Because they are made from organic ingredients, olive oil and Badger Balm produce less smoke and do not cause discoloration during the firing process like other types of oil, such as vegetable-based oils. Olive oil is also available in a spray, which can be used on large areas such as plastic texture sheets or large rubber stamps. Recently, new nonstick products made specifically for metal clay have also become available. They are sold under various brand names and are available from metal clay suppliers in spray or balm forms.

Spray Bottle

To keep clay moist as you work, sprinkle or mist it with water from a spray bottle. You can even dip a paintbrush or your fingers into water to join seams or to attach pieces of fresh clay. To prevent mold growth when storing opened clay that has been mixed with water, add a few drops of white vinegar to the water. Although tap water is fine to use, distilled water will help keep impurities and minerals out of the clay.

Roller

A lightweight plastic roller is helpful to roll flat sheets of clay. A plastic roller is less likely to stick than rollers made from other materials. A light coating of olive oil, Badger Balm, or other nonstick product will further minimize sticking.

Playing Cards or Mat Board

Spacers are good to use when rolling out clay sheets of various thicknesses. They act as a guide for the roller to keep the thickness of the clay consistent. Mat board is a good thickness for many projects and yields a nice, heavy gauge. Playing cards can also be used in the same way as a mat board. You can adjust the thickness of the clay by varying the number of cards stacked. Place a stack of an equal number of cards on each side of the clay to be rolled (see page 22). Playing cards can also be used as tools to move clay and to cut edges.

Craft or Paring Knife

Use a knife to score the clay, cut strips of clay, or cut out clay shapes. The tip of a craft or paring knife is ideal for drilling or enlarging holes in dried clay. My favorite cutting tool is a #11 X-Acto knife blade.

Tissue or Mat-Cutting Blades

Sharp, long blades are good for cutting nice straight edges. Polymer clay suppliers sell different types of blades, including wavy-shaped blades. Mat-cutting blades are shorter than tissue blades, but are more rigid and very handy for cutting edges. Mat-cutting blades are available at art supply stores.

Clay Shapers

Clay shapers are useful for repairs and for blending fresh clay into seams. Clay won't collect on shapers as it does on the bristles of a paintbrush. One end is a tapered, round shape, which is perfect for blending, sculpting, and making attachments, while the other end is a wedge shape to use for smoothing edges and pushing flat surfaces on the clay. I've found one I prefer above other brands due to the shape and type of rubber used for the tip. (In fact, it is called Sherri Haab's Favorite Clay Shaper—because it *really* is my favorite tool.) The firmness of the tool is just right for moving the clay. This particular tool is especially good for bronze and copper clays, which have a heavier texture than silver and gold. It's also useful for polymer clay as well. The clay shaper tool can be found on my website or from Metal Clay Supply (see Resources).

Paintbrushes

Small paintbrushes are useful for applying slip and water. A round, pointed paintbrush is good for smoothing and refining delicate, hard-to-reach areas. To cover large, flat areas use a wide brush. Stiff acrylic bristles are perfect for the texture of bronze and copper clays. The stiff bristles help to sculpt and smooth the clay. Softer brushes do not work as well, since bronze and copper clay is heavy and dense. I like the Winsor & Newton 233 University series size 3 or 4 brushes the best, because they work on any type of metal clay, including bronze and copper.

Needle Tool or Toothpicks

A needle tool is used for piercing holes, scoring, and making textures in the clay. It is commonly used by clay artists and can be found wherever you find ceramic supplies. Round toothpicks or large needles will serve the same purpose as a needle tool. Toothpicks can be fired, when needed to hold the shape of a loop or bead hole.

This clay shaper is my favorite tool.

Straws

Plastic drinking straws or small cocktail straws cut perfect holes in metal clay. Dip the straw in olive oil to prevent the clay from sticking to it. Straws also make good forms for tubular shapes and bails.

Plastic Wrap

Plastic wrap will keep unused clay from drying out. In addition to plastic wrap, I like to preserve clay using vacuum-type food sealer bags. With this type of bag, the vacuum sealer removes the air from inside it and then seals it. This type of sealer is especially good if you want to keep clay fresh for long periods between uses. Reseal the clay between each use. The vacuum-type bag also keeps paper or cork clay from drying out.

Small Containers

Small bottles, film canisters, and pill bottles are handy for storing extra clay, for mixing and storing slip, and for collecting scraps of dry clay. It is helpful to note here that you can recycle your clay by sending it to be reclaimed. Several large jewelry suppliers offer this service. Keep shavings, scraps, or even unwanted fired pieces in containers marked by the type of metal they contain.

Clay Cutters

Clay pattern cutters are available at art supply and craft stores. Klay Kutters are small metal cutters manufactured by Kemper Tools. They are available in a variety of shapes and sizes, and feature a plunger that pushes the clay out if it sticks in the cutter. They are often found with polymer clay supplies. I prefer stainless steel since, in addition to not rusting, the cutters will not affect the metallurgy of the clay.

Texturing Tools

The pointed tips of knitting needles, kitchen utensils, pieces of hardware, fabric, lace, buttons, and other found objects create great textures on clay. You can find metal- and leather-stamping tools at jewelry and leather supply stores. Rubber stamps made for paper can also be used to add texture to clay. Remember to oil rubber stamps well, as they will stick to metal clay.

Baby Wipes

Baby wipes are handy for wiping residue off your fingers. I find they work better than water because they keep your hands moist and prevent the clay from sticking to your hands. I sometimes place one over clay to keep it from drying out when I'm working and am too busy to wrap the clay between steps.

Emery Boards

These disposable fingernail files with two grits (one on either side) are great for all types of metal clay. Use them to refine the edges of your dried clay project prior to firing.

Brass or Stainless Steel Scratch Brush

Scratch brushes are used to burnish fired clay. I prefer a medium-soft brass scratch brush for most projects. The stainless steel scratch brush will keep copper or silver from turning gold in color when it is burnished.

3M Polishing Papers

3M polishing papers have a fine grit on a soft clothlike paper, and are used on both unfired and fired clay. Use the papers to sand unfired clay prior to firing, starting with the coarse grit and moving progressively finer. I use three grits: Green (400), Gray (600), and Blue (1200). After firing the clay, use the papers to bring the surface up to a high shine if desired. See page 26 for more information.

Curved Burnisher

A curved burnisher is used to burnish the raised areas or textures of the fired clay to add sparkle and shine. You could also substitute the back of a stainless steel kitchen utensil such as a spoon. In fact, any tool will work, as long as it is harder than the surface of the metal you are burnishing. Agate burnishers are also very popular with metal clay enthusiasts.

Pro Polishing Pads

Pro polishing pads are used to polish fired metal to remove patina or oxidation for a bright finish.

ADDITIONAL SUPPLIES

In addition to the basics, you may find a few specialty products that are helpful to use when working with metal clay. Metal clay suppliers offer supplies such as bead core materials, texturing tools, and firing devices—just to name a few. The following are my favorite supplies needed for certain applications and projects.

PasteMaker

Add a small amount of PasteMaker™ to clay to create oil-based paste or slip, which is used to make attachments and repairs. See page 24 for more information.

Cookie Cutters

Cookie cutters are an excellent alternative to clay cutters and can be found at your local kitchen or baking supplier.

Bead-Making Materials

Cork clay, paper clay, wood clay, and other bead-making materials are necessary for making beads and other hollow forms. Each material has certain properties that are compatible with the clay or technique used with it. Refer to the chapter about beads starting on page 63 for more information on which is most suitable.

Ring Forms

Premade ring forms such as HattieS Patties (see Resources, under Metal Clay Supply) or Redy Pellets (see Resources, under Cool Tools) ensure that the ring you make will fit after firing.

Molds and Texture Sheets

Molds and texture sheets are available in a variety of styles and materials. Some are made specifically for metal clay and do not stick to the clay as much as rubber stamps do.

Two-Part Silicone Putty

Two-part silicone putty is very easy to use and can be used to mold objects and then reproduce them in metal clay. It can be purchased from jewelry and craft supply companies.

Mandrels and Other Metal-Working Tools

Good tools are a must, especially for shaping, filing, and forming. I like the MultiMandrel™ set (see Resources, under Metal Clay Supply) for forming and sizing rings. Anvils, bracelet forms, hammers, and other tools are available from various jewelry-making suppliers and are helpful aids for finishing metal clay projects.

A few simple tools for working with metal clay include a roller, playing cards, work surface, stamping and sculpting tools, olive oil, and small cutters.

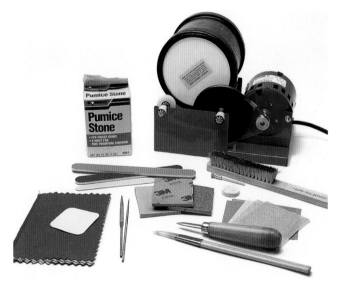

Finishing tools for metal clay include files, burnishing tools, sanding and polishing supplies, and a tumbling device.

Basic Techniques

Metal clay is unique in many ways, but its best quality is that it is very versatile, and as soon as you master a few basic techniques it is very easy to use to create jewelry. Once you get used to how the clay responds to moisture, how to form and sculpt on a small scale, and how to make attachments, you will be free to design dozens of projects with ease.

WORKING WITH AN OUNCE (28G) OF CLAY

In my workshops, many students are always amazed at how far a small amount of metal clay can go. When they see the small lump of clay in front of them, some students are afraid to get started while others fret about making just the right thing with a tiny, "precious" lump of clay I give them. I remind them that metal clay goes a long way and that if they make a mistake, they can always ball it back up and start over. One thing to keep in mind is that 1 ounce (28g) of copper or bronze clay is far less expensive than silver or gold.

A 1-ounce (28g) lump of clay is more than enough to make everything shown here: a bracelet full of charms, matching earrings, plus pendants and beads.

TERMS FOR CLAY STAGES

The following terms for various stages of workability from fresh wet clay to fired clay are good to know:

* **Damp, soft, or plastic clay:** This is clay that is fresh out of the package and is at the first stage of workability, allowing you to sculpt and texture the clay.

* **Leather-hard clay:** As clay dries, it starts to hold its shape in a rigid form. The term "leather-hard" is used in ceramics to describe this stage. The clay still retains a bit of moisture and can be scored or carved yet holds a shape. It can still be flexed a bit, but care should be taken not to break the piece.

* **Bone-dry clay:** This is clay that has dried past the leather-hard stage and is not yet fired. As clay is sanded and refined, it will produce fine dust shavings. It can be softened and rehydrated with water, if needed, to aid in repairs and attachments.

* **Greenware:** This term refers to dry, unfired clay pieces that can easily be attached to each other without losing their shapes. Slip or paste is needed to make attachments for greenware pieces.

* **Bisque:** This is clay that is fresh out of the kiln and has not been burnished or finished. The surface is very porous at this stage.

WORKING WITH METAL CLAY

As with any other type of water-based clay, there are various stages of workability as the clay dries. Sometimes fresh, moist soft clay is preferred for a technique, such as forming loops or pressing textures into the clay, while for others it helps to let the clay dry a bit so that it will firm up and hold its shape better, attaching formed elements, for example. Once you have become accustomed to the clay and how quickly it dries you'll become skilled at knowing when to add moisture as you work and when the clay is dry enough to move on to the next step. The changes in the clay's workability as it dries will vary depending on the warmth and humidity of your environment. There will be instances when you will want to speed up the drying time, and other occasions when you will need the clay to stay moist and flexible as you work. The advantages of dried clay are that it can be rehydrated and scraps can be used to make slip. In addition, metal clay can be recycled in this way, allowing nothing to be lost or wasted.

Keeping Metal Clay Hydrated

There are several ways to keep clay hydrated. Remove only small pieces of clay as you need them, keeping the rest in plastic wrap inside a sealed container with a small, damp sponge to prevent it from drying out. As you work with the clay, you can keep the consistency soft and pliable by incorporating water, either by periodically misting it with a spray bottle or by sprinkling it with water. You'll know when it's time to add water when the clay feels like chalk on the surface and cracks around the edges when rolled or pressed flat.

To hydrate the clay, press the ball of clay into a flat pad. Add a few drops of water into the center and then fold the clay into itself, which will blend the water into the clay from the inside out, preventing it from sticking to your hands. Roll it in the palm of your hands. Repeat a few times as necessary until the clay is a soft, workable consistency.

If the clay becomes too dry, add water and wrap it up for a

Keep your extra clay moist by wrapping it in plastic to prevent it from drying out.

few hours or overnight to rehydrate it. Bone-dry clay, or clay that is completely dry, may take longer, but it can still be reconditioned into soft clay. Oil or Badger Balm also helps keep your hands and clay from drying out while you work.

Silver and Gold Clays

Fresh, moist silver and gold metal clay right out of the package is easy to shape and manipulate. While the clay is soft and flexible, make delicate components such as loops, braids, and fine details at this stage. Pieces of wet clay can be attached to each other simply by applying water. Slip can also be used sparingly to join pieces of wet clay, but be cautious: Cleaning up slip around joins is tricky on fresh clay, as the clay piece will easily become misshapen or lose texture if it's too wet. With a little practice, you will learn to judge when the clay is firm enough to use slip.

Bronze and Copper Clays

If you're familiar with silver metal clay, you'll see that bronze and copper clays have a stickier texture and will stick to your fingers and tools. To help prevent this, oil your hands and fingers with olive oil or Badger Balm prior to working with bronze and copper clays. Oil your tools and cutters as well; this will minimize the amount of clay that sticks to them. If your clay is sticky right out of the package, take out a lump and let it sit for a minute or so to help reduce the moisture. Then you can pick it up and roll it into a ball. Or, if it is too dry and stiff to work with, add water and knead the clay to a working consistency.

It also helps to keep the clay cool as you work. Bronze and copper clays are very similar to cookie dough in that when chilled, the dough is firm and easy to handle, but becomes progressively stickier as it warms up. This is especially the case with bronze clay. As it becomes soft and sticky, try putting it in the refrigerator for a while in an airtight, Zip-lock bag.

Copper clay isn't as sensitive as bronze clay. The good news is that both bronze and copper aren't as expensive as silver, so don't worry if you lose some of the clay to "muddy" fingers. Just wipe it away as needed with a baby wipe and start over with clean hands. In addition, bronze and copper clays are different from silver and gold in that they don't self-adhere easily with water alone. Slip is required to make good attachments (see page 23). Since clay properties are subject to change as they evolve with new formulations, each may vary in texture and workability and may require adaptation on the user's part. For example, dry powder versions of bronze and copper clay by Hadar Jacobson allow the user the option to mix the clay to a desired consistency needed for a project.

TEXTURING AND SCULPTING

Being smooth and pliable, metal clay can be sculpted, textured, and stamped. Form shapes by hand or use small clay or cookie cutters. Form curved shapes while the clay is still moist. Blend simple shapes or formed clay components together to make more complex designs. Leather stamping tools, texture plates, and found objects can be used to texture the clay. Use olive oil or Badger Balm as a release agent to prevent tools or textured surfaces from sticking to the clay.

ROLLING SHEETS

Place a lump of metal clay on your work surface and use a roller to flatten the clay into a sheet. If the clay sticks, rub a small amount of olive oil or Badger Balm on the work surface and the roller. If the clay cracks and splits, it may be too dry. Mist the surface with water, knead the clay, and try rolling the clay again. If you see any air bubbles form as you roll out the clay, pierce them with a needle tool or toothpick and smooth the clay with your roller or fingers. Many of the projects in this book were made with sheets of rolled clay. The following two methods of rolling out create an even thickness:

Rolling Method 1

Roll the clay between two strips of mat board to get a thickness of about .06 inch (1.5mm). This thickness is sturdy enough for most metal clay projects, such as pendants, rings, or the wall of a vessel or box. From there, you can roll the clay into a thinner sheet by eye.

Rolling Method 2

Alternatively, use playing cards stacked for varying thicknesses, from a clever method developed by metalsmith Tim McCreight. Place the clay between the card stacks and roll it out. In the projects and techniques throughout this book, I will refer to a clay's thickness using this method. For example, when I recommend the sheet of clay be "four playing cards thick," it means that the clay sheet should be .06 inches (1.5mm) thick. The following is a list of playing card stacks and their corresponding measurements:

* two to three playing cards for thin sheets = .02–.04 inches (.5–1mm)
* four playing cards for medium-thick sheets = .06 inches (1.5mm)

Textures from a variety of found objects may be transferred to metal clay.

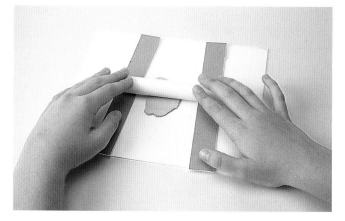

Rolling method 1

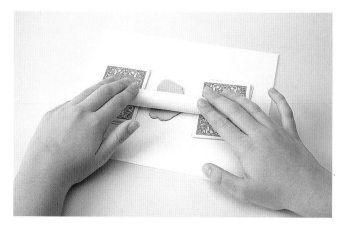

Rolling method 2

* five to six playing cards for thick sheets = .08–.10 inches (2–2.5mm)
* seven playing cards for extra thick sheets = .12 inches (3mm)

MAKING HOLES

Use a needle tool or toothpick to pierce holes in the clay to attach jump rings, wire, or stringing materials after firing. To avoid distorting the clay, make a small pilot hole with a needle tool or toothpick that will be refined later when the clay is dry. A drinking straw or cocktail stick can be used to make larger holes in the clay. Read about refining dry clay for how to enlarge and refine the holes before firing (see page 27).

MAKING ROPES AND LOOPS

Use fresh clay to make ropes, or "snakes." Thicker ropes can be used to make sturdy loops for pendants; very fine ropes can be used as decorative elements on a piece. To make a clay snake, pinch off a small amount of clay and roll it on your work surface using the fingertips of both hands. As you roll, move along the length of the snake, applying even pressure with your fingers for a uniform thickness. As you apply downward pressure, push or coax the clay away from the center outward to lengthen it. If the rope gets too long to manage, cut it into shorter pieces and continue rolling until you have the thickness you need. Spray the clay rope with water as needed to keep it moist. If you leave a rope of clay while working on another element, keep it covered with a wet towel, baby wipe, or plastic wrap.

To get a uniform thickness, use both hands and apply even pressure.

Attaching clay ropes or rings to unfired clay pieces eliminates the need to solder. To make a loop or small ring of clay, form a small, thin rope of clay into a circle. Cut the ends cleanly to make a butt join. Wet the ends with water and press together to seal. Let the loop dry a bit and attach it to the unfired metal clay piece with thick slip. Applying more slip or damp clay to the piece as it dries will ensure a secure bond.

ADDING ELEMENTS AND MAKING ATTACHMENTS

The following techniques will help you build forms and make attachments with various types of clay at different degrees of dryness. By adding clay attachments, you can build more elaborate pieces that structurally hold up well.

Attachments for Soft Silver and Gold Clays

When silver or gold clay is still damp, you can make attachments by simply adding water and pressing the pieces together. As soon as the clay is firm enough to handle, you can add attachments of fresh clay with slip, syringe clay, or water. The clay should be dry enough to keep its shape yet still have enough moisture to make the attachments adhere easily.

Attachments for Soft Bronze and Copper Clays

Bronze and copper clays do not self-adhere easily, so you'll need to make attachments by physically blending pieces of clay to one another using soft clay, paste, or slip. By simply using water for attachments, the clay will feel slippery and will resist sticking to itself. Make either a water-based slip or an oil-based paste to "glue" and attach the pieces. A good rule of thumb to remember is (1) use water-based slip to make attachments on damp pieces of clay, and (2) use oil-based paste for drier pieces. In both cases the slip or paste can be thick or thin, depending on the type of attachment you are making. With experience, you will quickly learn which method works best. To join seams, blend the clay firmly using a clay shaper to make a good mechanical connection with slip or paste between the seam areas.

Attaching Fresh Clay to Leather-Hard Clay (All Types)

If you're adding clay to a piece that's dry enough to hold its shape, use thick slip to make an attachment. Mix a medium consistency of slip and apply it to join the pieces. Press the pieces together using firm pressure to attach the clay. Blend the clay after making the attachment with a clay shaper tool.

Attachments for Dry Clay (All Types)

This technique will work for either leather-hard or bone-dry clay. To add an attachment, use the tip of a knife or needle tool to score the dry areas on either the base piece to which the fresh clay will be added or on the two dry pieces that will be joined together. Use oil paste to attach the pieces, let them dry, and then apply and blend the soft clay over the seam to ensure the attachment is strong. Use the clay shaper tool to blend the clay over the seam, followed by a round brush and water to refine the seam after it dries.

FILLING SEAMS AND GAPS

Wait until clay is leather-hard to fill gaps. Blend soft clay into the seam or gap with the clay shaper tool. Make sure the clay is densely packed into the gap and use a brush and water to refine prior to firing. Simply using slip to fill gaps will not be a sufficient substitute for dense clay, as it creates a weak bond due to a sparse metal particle density, which inhibits sintering

Homemade Slip

Slip is clay that has been watered down to the consistency of cream. Slip acts as a "glue" to attach either wet or dry clay elements to each other. You can buy premixed slip in paste form from metal clay manufacturers or you can make your own. Gold and silver slip are available in premixed formulas. Bronze and copper slip must be mixed as needed.

Making Silver and Gold Clay Slip To make your own silver or gold slip, mix dry bits of clay or unfired clay shavings with distilled water with a few drops of white vinegar in a small bottle or lidded container. The distilled water and vinegar inhibit mold growth and impurities in the clay. If you're in a hurry, you can mix slip right on your work surface with moist clay and water. Use a clay shaper tool to make a smooth paste or slip. Mark your slip jars so you'll remember which type of clay they contain. Always keep slip made with oil paste separate.

Making Bronze and Copper Clay Slip Slip is indispensable when it comes to working with bronze or copper clay. It's very easy to make and good to have on hand when working on a project. To make slip, use a clay shaper tool to incorporate water with the clay for a creamy paste. Start by making a thick slip, adding a few drops of water to a small lump of clay on your work surface. Blend well before adding more water until your desired consistency is obtained. Use the clay shaper tool to "mash" the

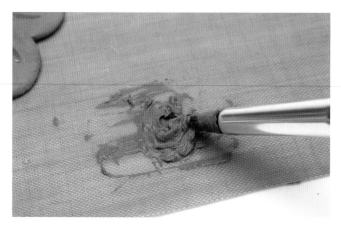

To make slip for bronze or copper clay, use a clay shaper tool to incorporate water into the clay until it reaches the consistency of soft frosting.

water into the clay until thoroughly blended. Continue adding water until it is the consistency of soft frosting. Slip can vary from thick to very thin, depending on what is needed for your project. Thick slip can be used to fill gaps or to make attachments. Thin slip, made with more water, is good for smoothing small cracks or refining rough areas. If you store bronze slip, you may notice a black film forming on the clay. This is the tin separating from the copper. Keep slip thick for storage, or make only as much as you need at one sitting.

Homemade Oil Paste

In addition to making slip with water, you can make an oil-based slip or paste that is stickier than water-based slip when making repairs. This is especially helpful for repairing previously fired pieces, and can be mixed for all types of clay. Many artists make their own pastes by mixing silver or bronze clay with lavender oil. I experimented with my own formulas and developed an oil-based mixture that I prefer over lavender paste. It is called PasteMaker, and is a bit stickier and is less likely to cause dermatitis.

To make all of my dry clay attachments, I use PasteMaker to mix my all-purpose glue, as it works great with all types of clay. Shake the bottle of PasteMaker well. Then mix six to ten drops of it into a small, pea-size lump of clay to a creamy consistency. If time permits, it's helpful to let the clay mixture sit in a closed vial or plastic container for a few hours, which allows the moisture to soak into the clay—so you won't have to spend as much effort incorporating water into it. Add a bit more water as needed until your desired consistency is obtained.

Using Syringe Clay

A syringe is perfect for working with either soft clay or slip, both of which are available in preloaded syringes. Syringe clay is soft clay that's perfect for making fine lines and ropes. It is particularly helpful when you need to cover or surround a large area with a fine rope, as the syringe offers more control than making a skinny rope by hand.

Syringe slip is a thinner formula than syringe clay, which is helpful to use when applying slip to joins. It's also less messy

container to prevent it from drying out. By adding a little white vinegar and water, you'll inhibit mold growth. Clays can be stored for months, but they may need to be reconstituted if they dry out. If mold appears, it will burn away during firing; but if mold is present, you should take precautions to protect your respiratory system with a mask while working, as mold spores are harmful to your health.

Measures can be taken to keep your clay as pristine as possible. While working on a project, keep the unused clay

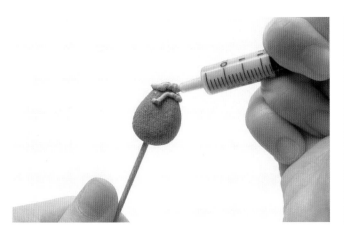

Syringe clay is applied to a bead core to make a lace pattern for a hollow bead.

You can reduce the time required to dry small metal clay projects prior to firing by using a warming device such as a coffee mug warmer.

than using a brush and easier to apply in tight areas or cracks. You can make your own syringe clay or syringe slip, but it's challenging to achieve the same consistency as commercial syringe clays.

To keep unused clay hydrated, keep the tip of the syringe submerged in a small jar of water. Florist's vials with rubber tops—the kind used to preserve a single flower—are perfect for clay syringe storage. You'll want to keep the clay hydrated, or clean it out of the syringe after each use—it'll be difficult if not impossible to remove if it dries.

STORING METAL CLAY

It's vital to properly store your clay to keep it from drying out, oxidizing, or becoming moldy. There are many methods to keep your clay in a soft, workable condition. One option is to store clay in containers filled with wet sponges, while another is to cover the clay with plastic wrap to ensure moisture retention. Wrap your metal clay in plastic wrap and keep it in a sealed

wrapped up tightly in plastic wrap. Press the air out of the clay's original Zip-lock bag as best you can, then seal it tightly. One of the best methods to remove air from packaging is a vacuum-type bag sealer commonly sold for food storage. This method will ensure that you'll remove as much air as possible in order to extend the life of the clay.

REFINING UNFIRED METAL CLAY

Be sure to dry metal clay pieces until they're leather-hard before refining them. Simply let them air dry, or use a warming device such as a candle or coffee mug warmer to speed the drying process. Small pieces are easier to dry with heat than large pieces. Large pieces may benefit from slow air-drying to prevent warping. Thorough, slow drying is especially important for larger bronze and copper clay projects. Trapped moisture causes bubbles to form on the surface during sintering. Nice, dry clay will sinter and fire more successfully.

Filing and Sanding Tools

Some of the tools mentioned for refining dry, unfired clay in this section can also be used to finish fired metal clay. See pages 41 to 43 for more information on how to use tools to finish the metal.

Metal Files Small, pointed files are used to finish rough or hard-to-reach places. Small jewelry files are available in sets from jewelry-making or model-making suppliers. File the surface in one direction only. Follow with progressive sanding to remove any scratches left by the file.

Emery Boards Emery board nail files can be used on unfired clay. I prefer small, inexpensive types with two grits on either side. Use the file to clean up the edges and to shape and refine the piece prior to firing.

Sanding Papers, Pads, and Polishing Papers 3M makes flexible, sponge sanding pads, graded from medium to microfine, to finish both unfired and fired metal clay. The medium grit is rough and will scratch the fired metal; it should be used if you're trying to remove a lot of metal or sanding a very rough area. Move progressively from coarser pads to finer grits to remove scratches and finish the metal for a smooth finish. Follow with polishing papers, if desired. Other types of wet or dry sandpaper from a hardware store can also be used to sand the finished metal.

3M Wet or Dry® Tri-M-Ite® Polishing Papers are thin, flexible sheets for extrafine polishing. These clothlike papers come in six different grits. You can cut the papers into small pieces that can be used to sand tight areas. You can create a mirror finish on metal clay by starting with the most abrasive paper and moving progressively to the finest.

The Refining Process

Use sanding papers or emery boards to refine edges and finish dry metal clay pieces as much as possible *before* firing. Although a metal file is often used after firing to remove rough areas, you can also use small metal files on unfired clay. Using files before firing saves you work and effort later on, as it takes more effort to shape and refine fired metal. Note that dry, unfired clay is fragile at this stage. Take care to hold and support the piece so that you do not cause any stress that could break it.

To sand and refine dried metal clay pieces prior to firing, use a small emery board with a coarse grit to remove rough areas. Use the finer grit to refine the edges and soften corners. Sanding papers or 3M polishing papers also work well to sand tight areas and curves. Copper and bronze clays tend to clog

Sanding and Polishing Papers

3M Sponge Sanding Papers come in the following grades:

* Medium
* Fine
* Superfine
* Ultrafine
* Microfine

3M Polishing Papers are color coded as follows, starting with green, the most abrasive grit, and ending with light green, the finest grit:

* Green
* Gray
* Blue
* Pink
* Mint
* Light green

Refine and finish metal clay pieces prior to firing with sanding papers or nail files.

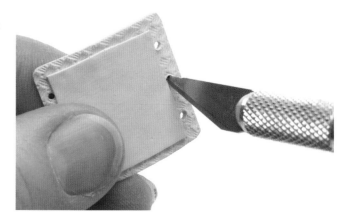

Use the tip of a knife to gently drill or shave holes in dry clay.

sandpaper and files more easily than silver clay. I like to use disposable files and sanding papers and then replace them as they become clogged with clay. Some wet/dry types can be cleaned with water, which helps, too.

To drill or shave holes in dry clay, use the very tip of an X-Acto knife blade. Place the tip of the blade into the pilot hole previously formed in the clay with a needle tool (see page 23 on making holes) and twirl the blade around until the hole is the desired size. Don't put pressure on the blade; use a soft touch to let it shave the clay evenly. If the clay is dry, the knife should produce fine dust and should carve or "shave" through the clay easily. Damp clay creates friction and the knife drags in the hole. If this happens, let the clay dry more thoroughly and then try drilling or shaving a hole again.

After you've sanded edges and refined holes, you can smooth any hard-to-reach areas with a small paintbrush and water. Be careful when removing textures with water; only a small amount is needed to soften the edges. Damp cosmetic sponges also work well to smooth dried clay.

DRYING METAL CLAY BEFORE FIRING

Although it's best to dry metal clay thoroughly before firing, silver and gold clays can be kiln-fired after minimal drying, and they will sinter even if moisture is present. However, they must be bone-dry when torch firing.

Bronze and copper clays, on the other hand, must always be bone-dry for proper sintering. Large bronze or copper pieces may take several days to air-dry entirely. Trying to speed up the drying process by warming larger pieces may warp them or dry the outside layer faster than the inside, giving you a false sense of readiness for firing. It's better to wait a few days rather than risk ruining a piece. If you fire a bronze or copper clay piece too soon and there's still moisture trapped inside, bubbles will form on the surface or you will encounter problems with sintering. Using a slow ramp speed—the rate at which the kiln heats up—will help bronze and copper clays dry more thoroughly and will avoid trapped moisture inside.

MAKING REPAIRS

Unfired and fired clay pieces can be repaired if broken. If your clay breaks prior to firing, brush water on the broken pieces and then apply slip. Press the broken pieces together and let the seams dry. After drying the clay, add another layer of slip, followed by an extra layer of clay to the backside of the piece (if applicable) for extra strength. This "patch" will help support the

repair. Smooth the clay with a clay shaper, or paintbrush, and water prior to firing.

Oil paste will help if you're having trouble attaching the pieces, as it has a stickier consistency than water-based slip. Always use a paste that is compatible with the clay you're using. You can buy premixed formulas, or you can mix your own with oil products made especially for metal clay (see page 24 for making your own oil paste). Oil-based paste formulas also work well to join fired pieces. Sometimes it's tricky to get water-based slip or paste to stick to fired metal. Add oil paste to adhere broken pieces, followed by a layer of fresh clay blended over the seams. Apply oil paste to unburnished metals for the best results. In addition to repairs, oil paste can be used to add new elements (fired or unfired) to previously fired and unburnished pieces. After the paste has dried thoroughly, fire pieces again.

Unfired clay can be repaired before firing by brushing water and thin slip onto the broken pieces, then pressing them together to dry.

While the piece is drying, you can add more slip to fill in any cracks that appear.

Firing Metal Clay

To properly sinter the metal pieces, metal clay needs to be fired long enough and hot enough so that the binder is burned away and the metal particles fuse. Underfired pieces are brittle and will snap like chalk. Overheating will melt the metal into a pool. You may observe this happening if you overheat when torch-firing. The metal will begin to shimmer like mercury as it starts to reach the melting temperature.

Each type of clay has different firing requirements and options. Refer to the firing charts on pages 36–39 to make sure you fire your metal clay pieces for the proper length of time and at the temperature specified for the particular clay. Bronze and copper clays require special conditions for firing; refer to the section about firing these metals on pages 38 and 39.

The firing times listed on the firing charts are minimums. It won't harm the metal to fire longer than is suggested, and doing so allows you to fire different types of clays together. However, if a project requires a lower firing temperature and it contains a stone or cork clay, for example, always fire the whole batch at the recommended temperature that the stone or cork clay dictates and long enough to sinter all types of clay during firing.

FIRING DEVICES

Small kilns, torches, and other firing devices that reach high temperatures to sinter metal clay are readily available wherever metal clay is sold. Just as metal clay products and accessories have been developed and improved since metal clay was first introduced, new firing devices, products, and methods have also evolved, making firing easier and less expensive than in the past. The type of clay used, the materials you'll be firing, and how many pieces you plan to fire will determine the firing device best suited for your needs. An overview of each type of firing device and its advantage follows.

Small Electronic Kilns

Following the rise in popularity of metal clay, suppliers began offering small kilns specifically for the purpose of firing metal clay. In fact, a few of these digital kilns feature preprogrammed settings with various firing schedules for metal clay. With the touch of a button, you can fire your clay without having to manually

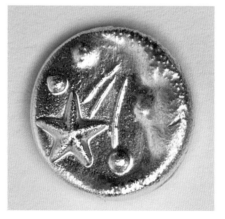

Both buttons were torch-fired. The one on the bottom was overheated. Notice how the detail of the moon was lost as the silver started to melt.

set the temperature and time. Most metal clay suppliers carry kilns and accessories, which makes the job of shopping for the right kiln much easier. Currently, a few companies feature very small kilns that contain the same features as other electronic kilns. They heat up quickly and weigh just a few pounds, making them perfect for travel or for the small studio. Even if the kiln isn't made specifically for metal clay, a programmable kiln is easy to use. Use the charts on pages 36–39 to manually set the temperature and time for the particular type of clay or project. If needed, set a ramp speed—the rate at which the kiln heats up.

Large kilns commonly used for ceramics, even if they have a controller, fluctuate quite a bit in temperature. The temperature and time need to be consistent for metal clay to sinter properly. A better solution would be to use a small enameling kiln outfitted with a pyrometer to kiln-fire the clay. Many metal clay artists successfully fire metal clay with this type of kiln.

Ultra-Lite Beehive Kiln This small electric kiln is an inexpensive alternative to a full-size electronic kiln. It can be used to fire lower temperature schedules for silver. It is also great for glass fusing and enameling. Accessories for firing and a temperature-control unit are available for use with this device, making it a versatile firing solution.

Lilly Kiln The Lilly® Kiln is a compact, lightweight electronic kiln. It has similar features to that of larger models with programs and temperature controls including ramp settings. The advantage to this type of kiln is that it heats up quickly, is lightweight, and fits in a small studio space.

FIRING SILVER AND GOLD CLAYS

The information in this section is *only* for silver and gold metal clays; bronze and copper clays must be prepared and fired under special conditions, which are explained on page 33.

Kiln-Firing Silver and Gold Clays

Prepare your silver or gold clay pieces for firing. Make sure that everything that's being fired together has a compatible firing temperature. Use the lowest temperature for a longer length of time if you're combining different types of clay or using materials that require lower firing temperatures.

Set the clay pieces on a hard Solderite™ pad (available from metal clay suppliers) or kiln shelf. The pieces can be touching since they will shrink when fired, leaving space

The temperature and time can be programmed with electric kilns specifically made for metal clay. This feature guards against overheating and other problems during firing.

The Ultra-Lite Beehive Kiln heats quickly and evenly, providing the ideal temperature for firing silver metal clay. The pieces should be completely dry before firing.

Small versions of electronic kilns are portable and heat up quickly, saving time and energy.

between each piece so they will not stick together. Round or shaped pieces need to be cradled in a fireproof material as they're fired. I prefer to use refractory ceramic fiber. Also known as a "ceramic fiber blanket" or "doll prop," it's used to make porcelain dolls and is available in ceramic stores. Some artists use other materials for supporting metal clay during firing. Small terra-cotta pots filled with vermiculite or alumina hydrate can be used to support round or dimensional objects. Vermiculite is commonly found in gardening supply stores, and is economical. Alumina hydrate works well to support pieces, as it is very fine and heavy; however, use caution with the loose powder. Because the powder is very fine and can damage your lungs if you breathe it in, you must wear a dust mask or respirator while using it.

Load the kiln with the shelves on which the metal clay pieces have already been arranged. You can use small kiln bricks to stack multiple shelves in the kiln. Place same-sized blocks in each corner for stability as you stack the shelves. Make sure that nothing is touching the thermocouple (the small probe sticking out of the back wall of the kiln that controls the temperature).

After loading the kiln, set the controls for the proper time and temperature needed to fire the clay. Refer to the kiln's manufacturer's instructions. After the firing is complete, unplug the kiln and let it cool down. You can either let the kiln cool slowly or open the door to cool it quickly. Leave the door shut if the project specifies a slow or controlled cooling time. Remove the shelves with hot pads or tongs. Pieces without stones or inclusions can be quenched in water to cool. Stones, glass, or ceramics may shatter if cooled too quickly, so let those materials cool slowly at room temperature.

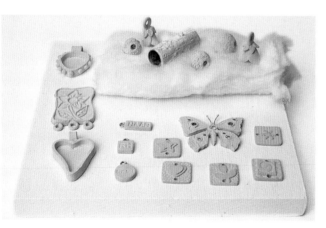

Round or shaped pieces need to be placed on extra support to retain their form and to keep them from rolling off the shelf. As shown here, flat pieces are laid directly on the kiln shelf, while a fiber blanket or "doll prop" is used to cradle round beads.

Ramp Speed

Firing temperature refers to the target temperature a metal clay requires for sintering. Ramp speed is the rate of temperature change per hour. For example, if you want to fire a piece at a firing temperature of 1000°, it will take two hours using a ramp speed of 500. Controlling the ramp speed is particularly useful when combining metal clay with materials such as glass, ceramics, and cork clay. Slower ramping reduces the stresses on metal clay or other heat-sensitive materials, resulting in fewer cracked, split, or ruined projects. The projects in this book give specific ramping instructions when necessary.

Kiln Safety

Be sure to follow these safety tips when using any type of kiln or firing device:

* Read the kiln manufacturer's instructions carefully before using your kiln.
* Do not fire the kiln hotter than is recommended for the metal clay.
* Do not leave the kiln unattended while firing.
* Do not touch the sides of the kiln while it is heated.
* Fire in a well-ventilated area.
* Do not bring anything into contact with the heating elements.
* Unplug the kiln after firing.
* Wear safety glasses when opening the door of a hot kiln.
* Always fire your metal clay items on a kiln shelf, not on the floor of the kiln.

Torch-Firing Silver Clay

Low-fire types of silver metal clay can be fired with a small handheld torch, such as the butane torches used to caramelize sugar for crème brûlée, instead of a kiln. Both the torch and fuel are available at kitchen supply stores. Torch-firing works for small pieces—those smaller than a large coin or projects made with less than .9 ounces (25g) of metal clay. You can fire clays such as PMC3, Art Clay Silver Standard, and Art Clay Silver 650/1200 with a butane torch.

Before you begin the following steps, make sure your piece is completely bone-dry. Place it on a firebrick or soldering block. Make sure you're working on a heatproof table and away from anything combustible. If a metal clay piece contains a stone, place the stone face down on the surface. Only use stones that are strong enough to withstand high temperatures. (For more information on firing with stones, see pages 76–79.)

1 Fill the torch with butane. Ignite the torch and hold it over the piece at a very close range, about 1¹/₂ inches (4cm) away.

2 Keep the torch moving slowly over the piece. A small flame and smoke will briefly appear as the binder burns out.

3 Keep the torch moving and watch as the piece glows red-orange. It's easier to see the orange color in a dark room, away from bright light or sunlight. Keep the metal glowing with even heat for proper sintering; at the same time, avoid melting the piece, which can happen quickly if you aren't paying attention.

4 As soon as the piece begins glowing red-orange, start timing. Fire for at least one and a half to two minutes after the red-orange glow appears. Large pieces can take a few minutes longer, up to five minutes. These are minimum times; it doesn't hurt to fire any piece longer. Keep the piece glowing orange the whole time, all the while moving the flame evenly over it. If the piece starts to shimmer or looks shiny, the silver is beginning to melt. Quickly pull the torch back. Continue firing, adjusting the torch distance as needed. After firing, turn off the torch and let the piece air cool.

Branch bracelets cast from a mold by Sherri Haab. Photo by the artist.

FIRING BRONZE AND COPPER CLAYS

Although both bronze and copper clays require special firing conditions that are similar to each other, the firing temperature needed to sinter copper clay is higher than that of bronze clay. Refer to the firing chart on pages 36–39 for more information on how to successfully fire both types of clay and fire mixed-metal pieces.

Because bronze and copper clays must be fired in a reduced oxygen environment for proper sintering, they both need to be fired between layers of carbon within a stainless steel container. The carbon absorbs oxygen as the pieces sinter. Both metals are sensitive to oxidation and will break or crumble if not fired properly. You'll need a kiln that has (1) a door or lid that keeps the chamber enclosed, and (2) heating elements that surround the walls of the chamber for even heating.

Bronze and Copper Firing Accessories

Bronze and copper clays are particularly sensitive to heat, so it's vital that kiln chamber temperatures stay consistent during the ramping and heating. The kiln can be brick or foam, top loading or front loading; however, *be sure the kiln you choose works for bronze and copper metal clays*. The kilns best suited to firing bronze and copper clays have heating elements within the walls of the chamber that allow the heat to evenly surround the container—rather than heating from just one source. Heating copper or bronze clays quickly or unevenly will over- or underfire a piece, as their sintering temperatures are very specific.

Stainless Steel Firing Container with Lid A stainless steel firing container is used to hold carbon that must surround the bronze and copper clay pieces during firing. Carbon is needed to accommodate for the oxygen-reduced environment. The lid helps keep the kiln cleaner as the carbon fires.

Coal-Based and Coconut Shell Carbon Coal-based and coconut shell carbon are two common types of carbon sold for firing copper and bronze clays. These products are used to absorb oxygen and to create an oxygen-reduced environment within the stainless steel firing container. To ensure you get the right type, it's best to buy carbon from suppliers who sell it specifically for metal clay. Carbon sold at pet stores or from other sources may inhibit sintering, as carbon varies widely both in texture and composition.

Because the quality of activated coal-based carbon varies from batch to batch, which may prevent copper clay from sintering properly, you should fire copper clay in coconut shell carbon, which seems to be more consistent in its quality.

Coal-based carbon produces a range of colorful patinas during firing, including blue, green, purple, and gold, while coconut shell carbon imparts pieces with golden hues. These colors may be left as is on the metal surface or burnished away during the finishing process. Carbon can be saved and reused for future firings.

Doble Flor Earrings by Lorena Angulo. Stamped BRONZclay with sterling silver wire. Photo by the artist.

Safety Note: For respiratory safety, make sure you *always* wear a dust mask when working with any type of carbon, as airborne carbon dust can get into your lungs.

Preparing Bronze and Copper Clays for Firing

Pour the coal-based or coconut shell carbon into the stainless steel container to make a base layer at least 1 inch (2.5cm) deep. Make sure the pieces are about ½ inch (1.5cm) apart from each other as well as from the sides of the pan. Cover each layer of pieces with at least a ½-inch (1.5cm) layer of carbon. Finish with a thick layer of carbon over the last layer of clay pieces, filling the container to the top. Cover the container with the lid.

Place the container in the center of the kiln, setting it on small pieces of firebrick to improve heat circulation. Make sure the container is not in contact with the thermocouple. Bronze and copper clays require consistent temperatures to fire properly. Make sure the kiln you use has a good controller with accurate temperature controls. Kilns with heating elements that surround the walls ensure even heating. Since some small kilns can spike in temperature as they heat up even if they are controlled, it's important to test-fire a few pieces. Underfired pieces will break, and overfired pieces will have a blistered appearance or even melt.

Firing Bronze Clay

Set the kiln to fire at a ramp speed of 250°F (121°C) per hour and hold at 1550°F (843°C) for three and a half hours. After the firing session, leave the clay pieces in the carbon to cool until they're cool enough to handle. If the pieces are removed from the carbon while they're still hot, they tend to oxidize quickly, turning black almost instantly—which can cause the pieces to break. Be patient and wait until the pieces are cool. Cooling bronze clay while it's still within the carbon will create beautiful patinas.

Once the pieces have cooled, remove them from the carbon and check for any splits or cracks. Beads and rings are particularly prone to splitting at seams. Fill any cracks, splits, or visible seams with oil paste or fresh clay. Let them dry thoroughly, refine as needed, and then refire.

Firing Copper Clay

Prepare the copper pieces as described on the previous page, but use coconut shell carbon rather than coal-based carbon. Set the kiln to ramp at full speed and heat to 1750°F (954°C) and hold at this temperature for three and a half to four hours. Leave the clay pieces in the carbon until they're cool enough to handle.

Alternative Two-Stage Firing Method for Bronze or Copper Clay

You might want to try this alternative method, which is a two-stage firing process. In the first stage, the pieces are briefly fired on a kiln shelf to burn off the binder in the presence of oxygen. In the second stage, the pieces are buried in carbon and then fired. This method is good for several reasons. The first advantage is that the binder can burn away without the presence of carbon during the first stage, which will ensure proper sintering by reducing the amount of oxygen that the carbon must absorb during the second stage. The result is that the pieces sinter to the center, especially with larger forms. The second advantage is that this method is good for bronze and copper beads and hollow forms. In addition, the two-stage firing method allows you to use combustible cores such as cork or wood, which burn out during the first stage. This results in less splitting caused by firing the clay around solid cores which do not burn away as the clay shrinks.

Fire bronze and copper clay in layers of carbon. The carbon will absorb and reduce the oxygen as the pieces sinter.

Start stage one by firing the pieces on a kiln shelf at a ramp speed of 550°F (288°C) per hour and hold at 550°F (288°C) for fifteen minutes. Because the metal is oxidized, the pieces will turn black and they'll be very fragile. When the pieces are cool enough to handle, prepare them to be fired again for stage two.

Start stage two by layering the clay pieces in carbon (as described in the Preparing Bronze and Copper Clays for Firing section on page 33) and fire at the appropriate firing temperature for the clay type. Bronze = ramp speed of 250°F (121°C) per hour up to 1550°F (843°C), holding for three and a half hours. Copper = full ramp speed to 1750°F (954°C), holding for three and a half hours. Although I have found success firing bronze at full speed, you can always ramp slowly to make extra sure the pieces sinter and to avoid cracks. (Many artists follow the traditional firing schedule of slow ramping after the open shelf firing.) As they sinter properly in a reduced oxygen environment, the finished clay pieces will lose their black color from the first firing and take on patinas created by the carbon.

Bronze and copper clay bracelets by Sherri Haab. Photo by Dan Haab.

Firing Copper and Bronze Mixed-Metal Pieces

Although copper and bronze clays can be combined to make mixed-metal clay pieces, they cannot be fired together in the greenware state. The copper clay piece must be fired first. The bronze clay must then be added to the unburnished copper. Finally, the whole piece is fired again at the bronze firing temperature. If both clays are fired together at the higher copper temperature, the bronze will overheat and melt.

Firing Silver with Bronze and Copper

Copper and silver can be fired together as long as the copper is fired first and the silver is then added to the fired copper. Silver does not fire well with bronze clay unless it is applied as a silver slip over prefired bronze pieces. Accent Silver is a product that is applied to clean, fired bronze or copper clay and then fired in an oxygen-reduced environment. Read the manufacturer's instructions for more information.

Patina colors on the surfaces of fired copper and bronze clay pieces range from pink to bright blue.

Above: If bronze clay is fired at a higher temperature than required to sinter copper clay, the bronze elements will melt as shown.

SILVER & GOLD FIRING CHARTS

The following silver and gold firing charts are a quick reference guide to help you select a firing schedule for your project at a glance. The guides show the sintering temperatures, time needed, and firing method required for successful silver and gold metal clay firings.

PMC Silver and Gold Clay Chart

PROPERTIES	FIRING TEMP/MINIMUM TIME	RECOMMENDED FIRING METHOD	SHRINKAGE
PMC Standard Good for small projects when shrinkage is desired; very smooth clay; good for charms, pendants, small sculptures	1650°F (899°C) for 2 hours	Kiln	25–30%
PMC+ Strong clay; good all-purpose clay for bracelets, earrings, pins, beads, cork clay, enameling	*1650° F (899°C) for 10 minutes 1560°F (849°C) for 20 minutes 1470°F (799°C) for 30 minutes	Kiln	10–15%
PMC3 Can be fired with glass, ceramics, and sterling silver findings (at lowest temp); good for rings and pieces requiring strength; can use with stones such as garnets, moonstones, and hematite	*1650°F (899°C) for 10 minutes 1290°F (699°C) for 10 minutes 1200°F (649°C) for 20 minutes 1110°F (599°C) for 45 minutes	Kiln or torch (see instructions on page 31 for torch-firing)	10–12%
PMC 22K GOLD Good for pendants, charms, earrings, rings; can be layered or fired with silver	1650°F (899°C) for 10 minutes 1560°F (849°C) for 30 minutes 1380°F (749°C) for 60 minutes 1290°F (699°C) for 90 minutes	Kiln or torch (see instructions on page 31 for torch-firing)	14–19%

*Note: Fire at 1650°F (899°C) for 2 hours for maximum strength.

Art Clay Silver and Gold Clay Firing Chart

PROPERTIES	FIRING TEMP/MINIMUM TIME	RECOMMENDED FIRING METHOD	SHRINKAGE
Art Clay Silver Basic Strong, all-purpose metal clay; good for pins, pendants, sculpted forms, beads	1600°F (871°C) for 10 min 1560°F (849°C) for 20 min 1472°F (800°C) for 30 min	Kiln or torch (see instructions on page 31 for torch-firing)	8–12%
Art Clay Silver Basic Slow-Dry Good for rings and detailed pieces; good in dry climates; allows longer working time	1600°F (871°C) for 10 min 1560°F (849°C) for 20 min 1472°F (800°C) for 30 min	Kiln or torch (see instructions on page 31 for torch-firing)	8–12%
Art Clay Silver 650/1200 Low firing clay; fires with sterling silver findings, glass, ceramics; can use with stones such as moonstone, garnet, and hematite	1472°F (800°C) for 5 min 1382°F (750°C) for 10 min 1290°F (699°C) for 15 min 1200°F (649°C) for 30 min	Kiln or torch (see instructions on page 31 for torch-firing)	8–9%
Art Clay Silver 650/1200 Slow-Dry Good for rings and detailed pieces; good in dry climates; allows longer working time; can be fired at lower temperatures than Basic Slow-Dry type	1472°F (800°C) for 5 min 1382°F (750°C) for 10 min 1290°F (699°C) for 15 min 1200°F (649°C) for 30 min	Kiln or torch (see instructions on page 31 for torch-firing)	8–9%
Art Clay Gold K22 gold	1813°F (989°C) for 60 min	Kiln	15%

BRONZE & COPPER FIRING CHARTS

There are many firing schedules available for firing both bronze and copper clays which have been developed and advocated by various artists. At the time of this writing, I have found the following schedules to be reliable which is consistent with the package inserts for the clays. New methods of firing the clays in multiple segments along with oxygen exposure introduced during the "binder burnout" stage are proving to increase the success rate for firing bronze and copper especially in regard to firing larger pieces.

Bronze Clay Firing Chart

PROPERTIES	FIRING TEMP/MINIMUM TIME	RECOMMENDED FIRING METHOD	SHRINKAGE
BRONZclay 89% copper, 11% tin; extremely strong; gold color			
Standard Firing Method	Ramp 250°F (121°C) per hour to 1550°F (843°C). Hold for 3½ hours.	Enclosed kiln; layer with carbon in stainless steel container	25%
Two-Stage Firing Method Two-stage firing is particularly good for firing beads and large pieces; can also be used for all bronze firings	**Stage 1** Ramp speed 550°F (288°C) up to 550°F (288°C). Hold for 15 minutes. **Stage 2** Ramp 250°F (121°C) per hour up to 1550°F (843°C). Hold for 3½ hours.	Shelf, kiln fire in closed kiln Enclosed kiln; layer with carbon in stainless steel container	
Hadar's Clay Quick Fire Bronze Powder form of quick fire bronze clay; shorter firing schedule than other types	Firing according to manufacturer's product instructions		10%

Copper Clay Firing Chart

PROPERTIES	FIRING TEMP/MINIMUM TIME	RECOMMENDED FIRING METHOD	SHRINKAGE
COPPRclay Red or warm brown color; good for large pieces			
Standard Firing Method	Ramp full speed up to 1750°F (954°C). Hold for 3½–4 hours.	Enclosed kiln; layer with carbon in stainless steel container	25%
Two-Stage Firing Method Open shelf two-stage firing is particularly good for firing beads and large pieces; can also be used for all copper firings	**Stage 1** Ramp speed 550°F (288°C) up to 550°F (288°C). Hold for 15 minutes. **Stage 2** Ramp full speed up to 1750°F (954°C). Hold for 3½–4 hours.	Shelf, kiln fire in closed kiln Enclosed kiln; layer with carbon in stainless steel container	
Art Clay Copper Strong copper clay; does not need to be fired in carbon	1778°F (970°C) for 30 minutes.	Shelf; fire in closed kiln; quench in water immediately after firing; soak in pickling solution to remove oxidation; follow manufacturer's safety precautions	20%
Hadar's Clay Copper Powder form copper clay; good shelf life	Fire according to manufacturer's product instructions		10%

STRENGTH CHARTS

PMC provides these charts to compare the varying strengths of
standard PMC with PMC+ and PMC3. Notice that PMC+ and
PMC3 don't require higher firing temperatures for strength.

Strength after Firing

| | weak | | very good | | pretty good |

PMC   Firing Temperature

°F	930	1020	1110	1200	1290	1380	1470	1560	1650
°C	500	550	600	650	700	750	800	850	900

Minutes

5									
10									
20									
30									
60									
120									

PMC+   Firing Temperature

°F	930	1020	1110	1200	1290	1380	1470	1560	1650
°C	500	550	600	650	700	750	800	850	900

Minutes

5									
10									
20									
30									
60									
120									

PMC3   Firing Temperature

°F	930	1020	1110	1200	1290	1380	1470	1560	1650
°C	500	550	600	650	700	750	800	850	900

Minutes

5									
10									
20									
30									
60									
120									

Finishing Techniques

Finished metal clay pieces will appear matte in color after firing. After kiln or torch-firing a silver clay piece, for example, it will have a powder-white surface color. A gold clay piece will have a light, matte yellow color that is not a coating, but the gold particles themselves in an unburnished state.

Using silver as an example: The matte white appearance of the piece is due to the way light reflects at all angles, which optically causes the silver to appear white in color (think of snowflakes). As the particles are burnished, or "flattened," the surface will reflect the bright silver. The more the surface is refined, the brighter and shinier the silver will become. After firing, the finished metal pieces are pure silver (.999), gold (22K), bronze (tin and copper), or pure copper.

The same traditional tools and techniques that are used to finish sheet or cast metal are also applicable for finishing fired metal clay, just with a few modifications. Fired metal clay is more porous than sheet metal, which means finished clay pieces will soak up patina or solder and must therefore be handled a bit differently to compensate for their porosity.

FILING

If you notice rough spots or uneven edges that need refining after firing, use a metal file to smooth the metal. Brace the piece on a wooden bench pin or rubber block and file the piece in one direction only until the rough spots or uneven edges are fixed.

BURNISHING

After firing the metal there are a number of techniques that can be used to refine and burnish it with various finishes.

Scratch-Brushing

Scratch-brushing is usually the first step, although sometimes the last, in finishing a metal clay piece. You will want to brush the clay piece until the metal starts to shine. One type of brush you can use is a scratch brush, which produces a satin finish. Small scratch brushes are available for flexible shaft tools for small areas. If you want a mirror shine, you'll want to follow up with fine sanding papers and burnishing tools.

While some artists brush metal with gentle soap and running water to lubricate the brush, I personally prefer to burnish with a dry brush. My favorite brush is a medium-soft brass scratch brush. Brass is good for burnishing all of the metal clays; however, it may impart a gold color to silver and copper. Stainless steel scratch brushes will help avoid this.

Jewelry suppliers sell brushes specifically for burnishing fine metals. Brushes from the hardware store may look the same, but are far too harsh and scratch the metal more than burnish it. Many of the projects in this book were finished with a brass scratch brush alone.

You can bring out the highlights of a textured piece by burnishing the raised surface areas. Go over the piece with a brass scratch brush until the metal starts to shine. Alternatively, you can use a stainless steel scratch brush for a similar matte finish.

Burnishing Tools

Stainless steel burnishing tools are available at jewelry and metal clay suppliers. Burnishing adds sparkle and shine to the raised areas on the metal. This is usually the final step in finishing a piece. Raised areas can be burnished with a hand tool immediately following scratch-brushing to finish a highly textured piece. If you choose to use sanding papers following

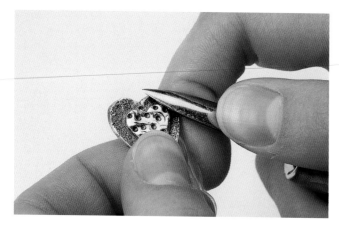

By flattening the metal particles, a burnishing tool adds sparkle and shine to the raised areas of texture. This is usually the final step in finishing a piece.

A professional-grade jewelry tumbler can be used to burnish fired metal clay.

scratch-brushing instead, then burnishing is the last and final step for a mirror finish. You can use common household items instead of a burnishing tool, such as knitting needles, stainless steel kitchen spoons, or paper clips, to burnish metal. They work especially well in tight spots.

To burnish an item, hold the piece firmly and apply pressure while rubbing on the surface of the metal with the tool. The tool will compress the metal particles for a high shine.

Tumbling

Another method for burnishing fired metal clay is to use a jewelry or rock tumbler. Choose a professional grade, not a hobby model. Jewelry supply catalogs and metal clay suppliers offer small tumblers, stainless steel–mixed shot, and burnishing compound. Mini-rotary tumblers are inexpensive and save a great deal of time if you plan on finishing a number of pieces.

Prepare pieces by scratch-brushing them beforehand. Fill the tumbler with shot and add enough distilled water to cover the shot by about 1 inch (2.5cm) along with a few drops of burnishing compound. Mixed shot consists of rod, sphere, and disk shapes. This combination of shapes allows the shot to burnish the surface of the metal, reaching all of the piece's nooks and crannies. Stainless steel shot costs more than steel shot, but it's worth the price because it doesn't rust. Hollow pieces, such as beads, can first be strung on a wire to prevent shot from being trapped inside.

Follow the manufacturer's instructions for operating the tumbler. Tumble the pieces for about an hour or two. After an hour, check the pieces periodically (every thirty minutes) and remove them when they reach the desired shine and finish.

Pieces begin to lose fine detail if they're tumbled for too long. Tumbling also work-hardens the metal for a stronger finished product.

SANDING AND POLISHING

After the metal clay is burnished with a brush, you can use the same sanding and polishing pads that are used to refine unfired clay (see page 26). Start with a coarse grit and progressively move to finer ones until a mirror finish is achieved. If you jump ahead and skip from a coarse grit to the finest, you'll leave scratches behind that are stubborn to remove. It's important to work through each grit before moving to the next grade.

PATINAS

The same surface treatments that are traditionally used on sterling, copper, and bronze can be applied to fired metal clay. This is true for changing the color or darkening the metal with patina solutions. There are solutions sold through jewelry suppliers that you can experiment with. Make sample chips of fired metal to keep a record of different patinas. Because fired metal clay is porous, it's best to burnish the piece well by tumbling or burnishing before soaking it in a patina solution. Unburnished metal soaks up the patina like a sponge, making it difficult to remove or polish the dark color from the surface of the metal.

A common method to change the color or darken pieces is to use liver of sulfur, available at any jewelry-making supplier. It darkens by oxidizing the metal. It can be used on silver, copper, and bronze clay; gold will not take patina. There are other chemicals and heat treatments that can darken metals.

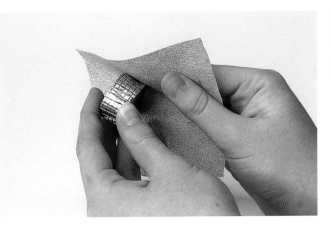

Create a mirror finish by starting with the most abrasive paper and moving progressively to the finest.

Use a wire to dip the piece into the patina solution.

Safety Note: Be sure to closely follow safety precautions when working with liver of sulfur. Work in a well-ventilated area with gloves to protect your skin. Liver of sulfur should be kept away from eating areas and be properly disposed after use. Check with local authorities on proper disposal methods in your area.

To begin the patina process, dissolve a few chips of dry liver of sulfur in hot water. Heat the piece, running it under hot water first. Use a wire to dip the piece into the solution and watch as the color moves from golden yellow to blue and finally to black-blue. Remove it from the solution when you like the color. Rinse the piece under cold water and polish with fine sanding papers and buffing cloths to remove the patina from the raised areas.

Liver of sulfur is also available in a gel formula that is resistant to oxidation. It's easier to apply and control than liquid liver of sulfur. It can simply be painted on at full strength or diluted for dipping pieces. This type of patina can also be shipped because it's nonflammable.

Black Max™ is an oxidizing solution that contains hydrochloric acid. It turns silver or copper black. Apply it to the metal with a cotton swab. Let the piece dry and then buff the raised areas with a polishing pad to remove the patina, leaving it in the recessed areas of the metal.

BUFFING AND POLISHING

After you have finished a piece with patina, buffing will restore the bright color metal from the raised areas leaving the dark patina in recessed areas only. Buffing pads and jewelry polish clothes are available through jewelry suppliers in various types.

My favorite pad is a Pro Polishing pad from Rio Grande. Pieces can also be polished using a rotary machine or flexible shaft tool fitted with muslin buffing wheels and jeweler's rouge to polish.

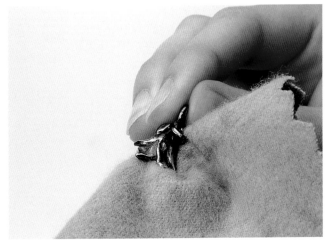

When your piece attains the desired color, rinse it under cold water and polish it with fine sanding papers and buffing cloths to remove the patina from the raised areas.

Metal Clay Techniques

texturizing, carving, & sculpting

One of the best things about metal clay is that it is extremely easy to texture with stamps (metal or rubber) and with found objects. Metal alphabet stamps can be found at hardware or jewelry-making supply stores. Rubber stamps and other texturing tools are sold at hobby and craft stores. Metal clay picks up every detail of a texture, which is retained after firing to reveal a smaller and more intricate version of the texture. Textures can be found anywhere. Experiment with fabric, lace, netting, screen, silverware patterns, buttons, or other household items. Objects from nature such as leaves, seed pods, branches, and seashells also make lovely organic textures. Even fingerprints can be featured textures!

Textures can be rolled or stamped into metal clay while the clay is still moist. A thin film of oil keeps the texturing tools from sticking to the clay. If the clay is too wet, the texture might smudge. If this happens, wait just a few minutes for the moisture to evaporate and then try applying the texture again. If the clay dries out too much, the texture will be faint. If so, brush or mist the clay with water and wait for a few minutes until the clay softens and try again. Unwanted marks can be either wiped away while the clay is damp or lightly sanded off after the clay dries.

Another way to add texture is to carve on dried, leather-hard metal clay. It takes a bit of practice to carve consistently and evenly, but it is very satisfying. It provides an alternative way of working with metal clay for those who do not enjoy sculpting. Carving metal clay is similar to the techniques used to carve stamps, woodblocks, and linoleum.

A more advanced technique of adding dimension and texture to metal clay is sculpting. One advantage of sculpting a design with metal clay is that you are not restricted by a complex design the way you would be using the traditional method, which requires you to sculpt the piece in wax first and then cast the piece out of metal. Sculpting allows you to skip these steps. Sculpted shapes can be simple or complex. Complex pieces are simply made by combining smaller shapes together in stages, building one form upon another. It is liberating to sculpt with metal clay, especially with textured designs with undercuts (places that would otherwise catch in the mold if they were sculpted in wax).

Whether stamped, carved, or sculpted, textures add depth and interest to a metal clay piece. After the clay piece has been fired and finished, you can enhance the surface to make the texture stand out. Bring out the highlights by burnishing the raised surface areas using a burnishing tool or agate on the raised spots. The shiny burnished surface will then contrast with the duller recessed areas. Another way to bring out a texture is to darken the recessed areas. Use a patina on the metal as directed on page 42. Buff the raised areas to bring back shine. These surface treatments will add depth and provide contrast to the surface of the textured clay for a rich look.

Creating Simple Textures

Use lace, textured stamps, even your fingerprints to texture metal clay to make dainty charms. Standard PMC is a good choice for making charms, because it shrinks more than the other clays and allows for tiny details. Regular PMC should be fired in a kiln for maximum strength. You can also make charms out of any other metal clay types following the manufacturer's instructions.

MATERIALS YOU'LL NEED
FOR A CHARM BRACELET:

Metal clay—any type
Basic metal clay tools (*see pages 16–18*)
Leather stamping tools
Lace, screen, or found objects for
    texturing
Small cookie cutters
Charm bracelet
Jump rings
Flat-back rhinestones (*optional*)
Quick-setting mold (*optional,*
    see pages 56–62)

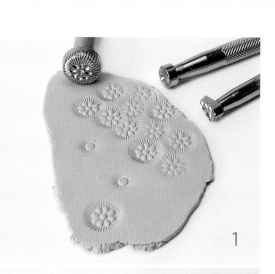

1   Roll out a .05 inch- (1.5mm) thick sheet of silver clay about four playing cards thick. Texture the clay with leather stamping tools, lace, screen, or a found object.

2   Cut out shapes with small cutters to make charms. Use oil to keep the cutters from sticking.

3   Layer smaller shapes onto larger ones to add dimension to some of the charms. Use water or thin slip to attach one shape onto the other. Press lightly to adhere. You can attach other elements such as small clay balls or ropes using slip for even more detail.

4 Pierce holes at the top of each charm using a needle tool or a small cocktail straw. Let the charms dry on a flat surface or warming tray.

5 After the charms are bone-dry, smooth the edges with a nail file or sanding papers. Clean, refine, or enlarge the holes using the tip of a knife. Be sure the holes are large enough to allow jump rings to pass through after firing.

6 Fire the charms flat on a kiln shelf as directed for the type of clay you are using. Finish the charms with a brass scratch brush. Use polishing papers or a burnishing tool to highlight the raised areas for even more shine. For extra flair, glue rhinestones onto the finished charms with quick-setting mold.

Attach the charms to a purchased charm bracelet with jump rings.

Sculpting Simple Shapes

The key for successful sculpting is to keep the metal clay moist as you work. In this project, a simple shape is used to sculpt a rose pendant. Use plastic wrap to cover the clay as you assemble the rose. You can sculpt other types of flowers by simply changing the shape of the petals. The more petals you add, the more detailed the flowers appear. Look at different petals in nature for inspiration.

MATERIALS YOU'LL NEED
FOR A ROSE PENDANT:

PMC Standard, or other silver metal clay
Basic metal clay tools (*see pages 16–18*)
Cord for pendant

1 Pinch off a small ball of clay and flatten it between your fingers to make a small, flat oval shape. Roll the oval into a coil to make the center of the rose.

2 To make the rose petals, roll pieces of clay into balls and then flatten them. Form each flattened ball into a wide teardrop shape. Make six to ten petals, depending on how big you want to make the rose. Start with smaller pieces and make them bigger as you add petals.

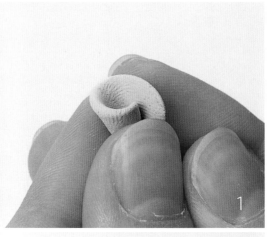

3 Using water to adhere, add the first petal with the pointed end down, pressing it to the center coil. Continue to attach each petal by overlapping each one over the last. Use water and a clay shaper tool to firmly attach the clay petals to each other. Keep adding petals until you like the size of the rose.

4 Use a blade to slice off the back of the rose to reduce the bulk and to flatten the back.

5 Let the rose dry. In the meantime, make the loop. Roll a piece of clay into a rope. Bend the rope into a loop and attach it with slip to the rose. You can add more slip as the piece dries for a secure bond and fix any flaws at this stage.

4   5

Fire the rose pendant on a kiln shelf (PMC Standard = 1650°F [899°C] for two hours or as directed by type of silver metal clay). Use a brass scratch brush to finish the rose after firing. Hang the pendant from a cord to make a necklace.

Fire on a flat kiln shelf (PMC Standard = 1650°F [899°C] for two hours). Use a brass scratch brush followed by sanding papers, working progressively to the finest grit for a smooth shine. Finish the pieces with a patina to darken the recessed areas (see page 42). Polish the raised areas with a buffing cloth to restore the shine. Hang the pendant from a leather cord or beaded chain.

Textured, Carved & Sculpted Metal Clay

top: *Pajaro Pendant* by Lorena Angulo. Hand sculpted BRONZClay with turquoise bead. Photo by the artist.

top right: *Magnolia Cuff* by Nancy Hamilton. PMC3 and Aura 22 on hand-woven sterling silver cuff with PMC ends. Photo by the artist.

bottom right: *Windhouse* by Catherine Witherell. Hand-constructed and sculpted PMC+, sterling silver chain and wire, pearl, tourmaline, and spinel. Photo by the artist.

working with molds

Making molds is addictive. Serious clay artists carry mold-making materials with them on their travels in case they should stumble upon interesting textures to cast, such as an old doorknob, button, or seashell. A mold will pick up fine details and does not stick to most materials.

Flexible molds can be made with two-part silicone putty compounds, which allow you to flex and bend the mold to release the cast clay object. Flexible molds allow for intricate details and some undercuts. Silicone molds cure at room temperature. There are several brands on the market to choose from, including Cold Mold™, EasyMold®, Equinox® 35 Fast, and Silputty®, which are available through antique restoration or jewelry supply companies. The formulas mentioned here mix at a 1:1 ratio and are extremely easy to use. In addition, they cure in a relatively short time and do not require a release agent when molding a piece of clay.

Bronze Tree of Life Pendant by Christina Leonard. Bronze patterned with hand-carved press mold. Photo copyright © by Jonathan David Sabin.

Simple Molds

Two-part silicone molds are a quick and easy way to make molds. They set up quickly and are flexible. You can mold intricate pieces that will pop out easily because of the mold's flexible properties—a great way to replicate antique treasures for jewelry making.

MATERIALS YOU'LL NEED FOR SHANK BUTTON:

PMC+, or any other metal clay

Basic metal clay tools (*see pages 16–18*)

Buttons to mold

Two-part silicone mold compound

1 Start with an equal-sized ball of each part of the silicone putty components. Knead and mix the components well, until the putty is one solid color. Work quickly, as the putty cures quickly.

2 Quickly press a button into a pad of the mixed putty. Let the button sit in place until the mold has cured.

3 Remove the button from the mold.

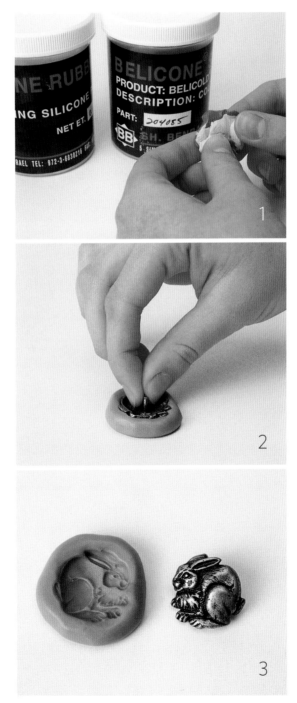

4 Press the metal clay into the mold. Flex the clay out onto a work surface or let the clay dry in the mold. It should release easily from the mold in either case, providing the clay is not too moist.

5 Roll a thin rope of metal clay to make the shank. Form the rope into a U-shape and trim the ends to make them blunt. Let the shank dry.

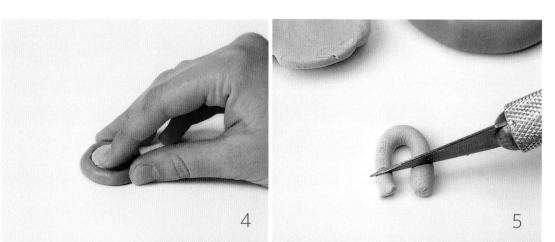

4

5

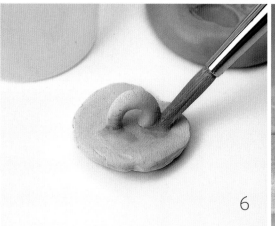

6

6 Attach the metal clay shank to the back of the molded–metal clay button with thick slip.

Fire the buttons as directed by the type of clay used. Finish the buttons with a brass scratch brush until desired shine is obtained.

Casting an Object Using a Two-Part Mold

By making a two-part silicone mold, you can replicate three-dimensional objects such as this antique key. Look for objects without undercuts. This project uses bronze clay, but you could use any metal clay you like. Silicone doesn't stick to metal clay, but it must be oiled so that it does not stick to itself when making two-part molds. There are many brands of silicone putty available, each with different curing times. Some cure within three to five minutes, while others take thirty minutes or longer to cure. They also vary in shore hardness, which describes how soft the rubber feels after curing. I use putty formulas that mix at a 1:1 ratio for their ease of use.

MATERIALS YOU'LL NEED FOR AN
ANTIQUE MOLDED KEY:

Metal clay, any type (*bronze clay was used in this project*)
Basic metal clay tools (*see pages 16–18*)
Antique key, or other object to mold
Two-part silicone mold compound
Pointed tool
Olive oil
File, or other finishing tools
Patina (*optional*)

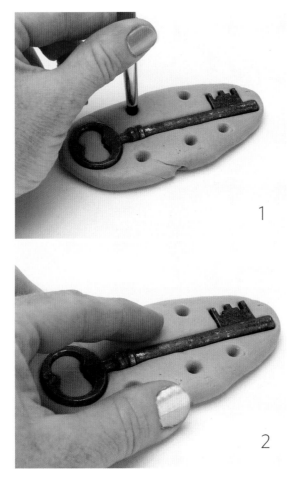

1 Mix the two-part silicone putty compounds as directed on page 57. Mix enough compound to make half of the mold for the object you are casting. After the compound putty is thoroughly mixed, work quickly to flatten it. Press the object (in this project, an antique key) into the mold putty. Press half of the thickness of the key into the mold. Make holes using a pointed tool around the object; they will act as registration marks for the mold.

2 While the putty is still soft, push the putty in and around the object, making sure there are no gaps around the edge.

3 Let the putty set until cured. Test by pushing your fingernail into the putty. If no mark remains and the putty springs back, it is cured. Brush the entire surface, including the holes, with a thin layer of olive oil. This will prevent the next layer of putty from sticking, so you can open the mold.

4 Mix another batch of putty, the same amount as you did for the bottom layer in step 1.

5 Press the mixed-putty mold over the top of the cured layer, leaving the object in place to be enclosed inside. Press firmly to make sure the mold has good contact with the registration marks and the object below.

6 After this top layer cures, you can pull the layers apart and remove the object from the mold.

7 To form the metal clay using the mold, shape the piece to fit roughly into the mold cavity. It is good to keep the clay in one piece so that you won't have seams or weak areas, which might break later. Press the clay into the bottom layer of the mold.

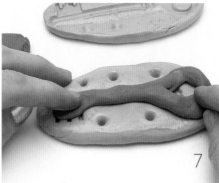

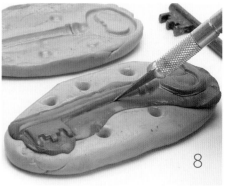

8 Press the top layer of the mold over the clay. Press firmly, making sure the registration marks line up and that the mold layers are in full contact. Remove the top layer of the mold and trim the excess clay away with a knife. Repeat and press the clay a second time, to make sure the clay is formed. You may have to trim more clay that is displaced away, especially if the mold was full of clay to begin with.

9 Let the object dry in the bottom half of the mold until it sets a bit. Carefully remove the object by flipping the mold over and flexing it to release the clay piece. Continue to let the clay dry until leather-hard. Refine the edges of the clay with a file to remove the seam that was left by the mold.

After the clay is refined, let it dry until bone-dry, especially if using bronze or copper clays. Fire the clay according to the type of clay used. Finish by burnishing, or tumbling, or leave it as is. Add a patina if desired.

Cast Metal
Clay Jewelry

left: *Peony Pin* by Catherine Witherell. Cast fine silver from a handmade mold by the artist. Photo by the artist.

above: *Wing* by Lisa Blackwell. Cast bronze from an original mold made by the artist. Photo by the artist.

beads

A bead core is needed to form and hold the shape of a metal clay bead while it is being fired. Various materials such as cork clay, cold cereal shapes, wood clay, and twigs can be used to make bead cores. Some materials are combustible, which means they will burn away during the firing process. Bisque ceramic beads and cores made of Paperclay® are two bead core materials that don't burn away. Cylinder-shaped drinking straws are also a good choice for forming beads, which can be removed prior to firing.

Cork clay is excellent for making your own bead cores, as it will hold the shape of the clay bead yet burn away during firing. It's easy to mold the cork clay into any shape. When it dries, it makes a lightweight bead core. Cork clay needs to be completely dry before firing. A light coating of white PVA glue (Sobo works very well) helps to seal the beads and helps the metal clay to stick to the core.

Loose Beads by Catherine Witherell. Hand-constructed and sculpted hollow beads with PMC3. Photo by the artist.

Some materials are dangerous to fire with an open heat source because they emit smoke and fumes. Cork clay is one of these; therefore, it should only be used on projects fired in a closed kiln. Some of the smoke may escape from the kiln, so work in a well-ventilated area. Always fire silver clay beads made with cork clay at 1472°F (800°C) and at a ramp speed of 1500°F (816°C), as cork clay burns hot and may cause silver clay to melt if fired at higher temperatures. To fire cork clay with copper and bronze clays, follow the two-stage firing charts on pages 38 and 39.

Metal clay can be applied directly to the surface of cork clay. Unused cork clay needs to be stored in an airtight package, such as vacuum-type bags that are made for preserving food, to keep it from drying out.

Another option for making bead cores is wood clay, which is similar to cork clay in that it is molded, dried, and burned away during firing. It's smoother in texture and sands and drills nicely, with less crumbling than cork clay.

Creative Paperclay is a material that is made with fine, volcanic ash. It won't burn away during firing. Creative Paperclay can be used when you want the metal clay bead to shrink as little as possible. The metal clay surrounding the bead core will thin as it shrinks, so make sure you account for this by keeping the metal clay loosely wrapped around the bead core to allow for the shrinking.

Drinking straws work well for piercing holes in beads, especially small, cocktail-size straws. Needle tools can be used to form smaller holes. Holes can be enlarged and refined after the clay beads are bone-dry. For fancy beads, use texturing tools to decorate while the clay is still wet. Techniques and applications for other projects in this book can be applied to beads.

beads

Cork clay is an excellent material for making bead cores that support metal clay bead shapes during firing. But because of the toxic fumes it emits, do not torch-fire beads made with cork clay.

Creating Round Beads

Round beads can be used as part of a larger design or as a single element of design. Art Clay Silver is a sturdy, all-purpose clay that works well for making round beads. You can also use other types of clay if you account for the firing temperature of the bead core material. To make copper and bronze beads, follow the two-stage firing charts on pages 38 and 39, which allows you to use combustible bead cores with those clays.

**MATERIALS YOU'LL NEED
FOR ROUND BEADS:**
Art Clay Silver Basic
Basic metal clay tools (*see pages 16–18*)
Cork clay
Sobo, or PVA white glue
Needle tool, or small cocktail straws
Texturing tools, or leather stamping tools

1 Make round cork clay bead cores. Let the cores dry in a warm place or in a dehydrator until thoroughly dried. Coat with a thin layer of glue to seal the beads. Roll out a sheet of metal clay about three playing cards thick. Cut a strip of clay long enough to wrap around the circumference of the bead and wide enough to cover the bead's height.

2 Cover the bead core with the clay, cutting away any excess clay from the top and bottom with a knife. Use slip and water as needed to join the seams, smoothing the clay until the bead is completely covered.

3 Decorate the bead with leather stamping tools.

4 Use the needle tool or small cocktail straw to make a hole on each end of the bead. Remember, the core burns away during firing, leaving a hollow bead.

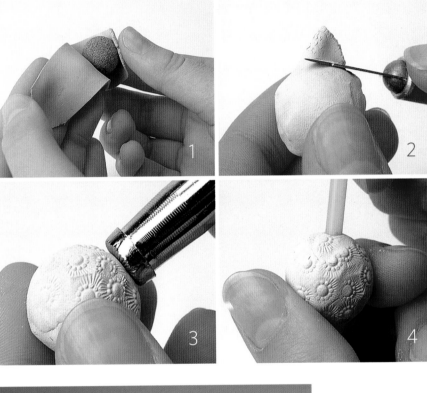

Lay the beads on a bed of fiber blanket on a kiln shelf and fire (Art Clay Silver = 1472°F [800°C] for thirty minutes). Finish the cooled beads with a brass scratch brush, using a burnishing tool to highlight the raised areas.

Creating Tube Beads

Tube- or cylinder-shaped beads look great strung on a fiber or leather cord. Ready-made beads often have small holes, which can be frustrating when looking for the perfect bead to fit over a cord. With metal clay, you can create tube beads around cores of any size to accommodate your stringing project.

MATERIALS YOU'LL NEED
FOR TUBE BEADS:
Art Clay Silver clay
Basic metal clay tools (*see pages 16–18*)
Plastic drinking straw
Leather stamping tool, or other
    texturing tool

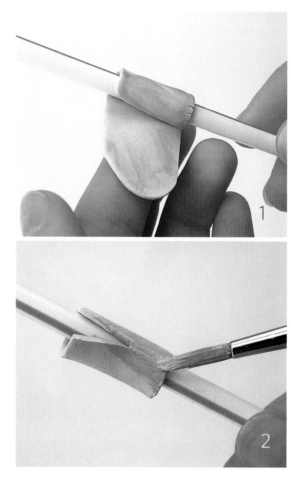

1 Roll out a sheet of metal clay about three playing cards thick. Use lace, screen, or silverware to texture the surface if desired. Cut the textured clay into strips and wrap one strip around a drinking straw (textured side out).

2 As you wrap the clay around the straw, you can leave a mark on the clay to indicate where it should be trimmed. Use water and thin slip to form a butt join at the seams.

3 Add details to the beads by adding small balls of fresh clay. Attach the clay with water and thin slip. Press the balls of clay with a leather stamp to decorate. Let the beads dry until firm enough to hold their shape on the straw.

4 Remove the straws by gently twisting the beads off. Let the beads continue to dry until bone-dry. Sand the ends of the beads. Sand in a circular motion on a piece of sanding paper or use a nail file to smooth the edges.

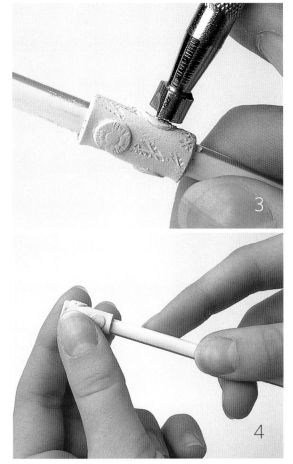

Lay the beads on a bed of fiber blanket on a kiln shelf. Fire the beads according to the manufacturer's instructions. Finish the cooled beads with a brass scratch brush, using a burnishing tool to highlight the raised areas.

Creating Beads Around Silver Cores

Create one-of-a-kind interchangeable beads designed to fit the popular Pandora- or Troll-style chains. These beads feature a fine silver core that's threaded inside to fit perfectly over a chain bracelet or necklace. The beads also look great strung on leather. Surround the bead cores with fine-silver clay to form the beads using a variety of techniques. Sculpt detailed designs, emboss with texture, embed stones, stamp with letters, or add birthstone bead dangles to the clay beads. The core is fine silver, which fires perfectly with metal clay, and adds a refined look to your finished clay beads. After firing the beads, you can finish them as desired. Use clays with low shrinkage rates for optimal success. Copper and gold clays can be fired over fine-silver cores, but bronze clay may be problematic.

MATERIALS YOU'LL NEED FOR TINY
SILVER-STUDDED BEADS:
PMC3
Basic metal clay tools (*see pages 16–18*)
8mm flared bead cores with threads
    (*available from Metal Clay Findings,
    see Resources*)
2mm silver balls (*available from Metal
    Clay Findings, see Resources*)
Tweezers

1 Pinch off a small piece of clay and roll it into a log shape that is long enough to wrap around the silver core finding. It is important that you wrap the clay loosely around the core, as the clay will shrink as it dries. It will shrink further during the firing process.

2 Smooth the seam and shape the clay with your fingers around the core. Make sure the clay is distributed evenly around the core.

3 Smooth and dampen the bead with water using a brush. This will help the balls to adhere and keep the clay from drying and cracking.

4 Use tweezers to push each silver ball into the clay to form a pattern around the bead; the ball should be deep enough so that half of the ball is embedded.

5 As the clay dries, use a brush and water to apply slip around each ball. This will help to secure the attachments and neaten up the surface.

6 Let the bead dry. Watch for cracks and repair as needed; fix by adding more clay or slip. Smooth the surface with water. When the beads are thoroughly dry, they will be ready to fire. Set the beads vertically (for support) on the kiln shelf, or you can rest them in a bed of fiber blanket or other fireproof support. The beads can be fired using any method recommended by the type of clay you are using. This photo shows how the beads appear after firing.

7 After firing and cooling the beads, brush them first with a brass scratch brush. This photo shows a soft-bristled brass scratch brush, which will burnish the silver to a nice matte finish.

8 To burnish the textured details on the surface of the beads, rub the heel of a burnishing tool over the bead. This will compress the silver particles, bringing the raised texture to an instant shine. You can also mechanically burnish the beads in a tumbler filled with stainless steel shot, distilled water, and burnishing compound. The pieces may be put into the tumbler immediately after brass brushing. Leave them in the tumbler for about one hour, or until the desired finish is achieved. If a patina is desired, follow the steps for the letter bead variation (see page 71).

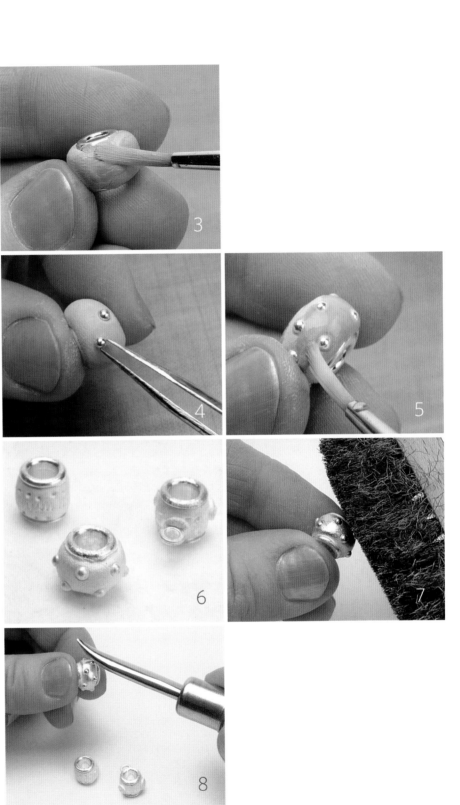

Faceted crystal bead

Eye pin

Head pin

4mm embeddable jump ring (*available
from Metal Clay Findings, see
Resources*)

Leather stamping tool, or other
texturing tool

Round-nose pliers

Chain-nose pliers

1 Surround a bead core with clay
following steps 1–3 for the Tiny Silver-
Studded Beads on page 68. Form balls of
clay to decorate the surface and attach
them with slip. Press the balls flat and
stamp a design using a leather stamping
or other texturing tool to make textured
designs on the bead.

2 Press an eye pin into the clay,
embedding the end deeply into the
center of one of the textured designs.

3 After firing, burnish the bead, then
add a patina if desired. To add a
bead drop, thread a bead onto the ball
end of a head pin. Form a wire loop out of
the head pin with round-nose pliers at the
top of the bead.

4 Attach the wire loop to the fired
bead.

5 Hold the wire loop with the tip of
chain-nose pliers. Wrap the end of
the head pin wire around the base of the
loop a few times.

6 Clip off the excess head pin wire
close to the bead. Tuck the end
of the wire in and under the wrapped
section with the tip of chain-nose pliers.

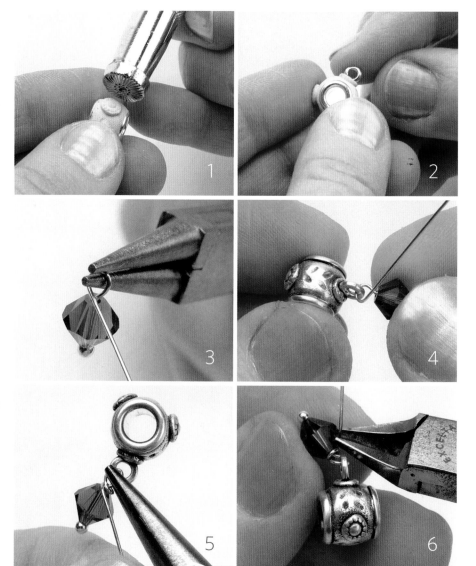

Metal or rubber letter stamps
Patina and silver polishing pad (*optional*)

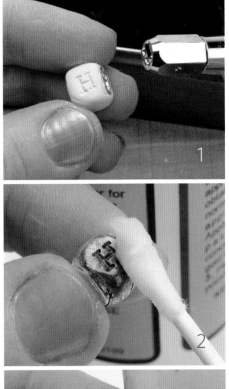

1 Surround a bead core with clay following steps 1–3 for the Tiny Silver-Studded Beads on page 68. Shape the clay into a cube around the bead core to give you four flat sides to apply letters. Stamp letters on each clay surface of the bead using metal or rubber stamps. (If you're using rubber stamps, oil them first with olive oil to prevent sticking.) Let the bead dry; smooth out any imperfections around the letter with a brush and water, working gently to avoid "wiping out" the stamped design. Let the bead dry before firing. Fire the bead and cool.

2 Use a cotton swab to apply a patina to emphasize the details of the letter.

3 After applying the patina, wipe the patina off the raised areas with a silver polishing pad.

Alpha Beads by Michelle Haab. Hand-sculpted beads over fine silver cores. Photo by Sherri Haab.

Four 4mm round fine-silver bezels
(look for Open-Back Bezel Settings from
Metal Clay Findings, see Resources)
4mm round cabochon stones
Burnishing tool or bezel pusher

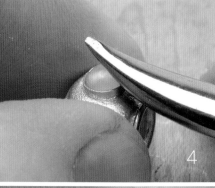

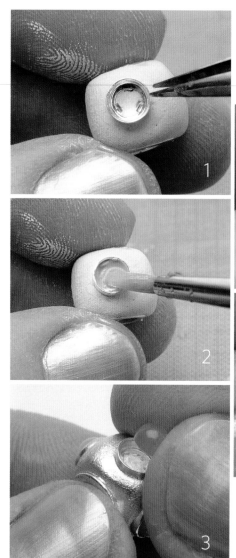

1 Surround a bead core with clay following steps 1–3 of the Tiny Silver-Studded Beads on page 68. Shape the clay into a cube around the bead core to give you four flat sides to add the bezels to. Use tweezers to push the bezel into the surface of the clay, making sure the prongs are embedded deeply into the clay (to secure the bezel). Repeat the process and add a bezel to the other three sides.

2 Let the bead dry enough to handle without misshaping. Use a brush and water or thin slip to cover the inside area of the bezel, making sure the bezel's prongs are covered.

3 Fire the bead and burnish as desired. To add stone cabochons (chalcedony stones were used here), set a stone into the first bezel. Make sure the stone fits properly without any interference.

4 Using a burnishing tool or bezel pusher, push the sides of the bezel in and around the stone. To properly push the sides of the bezel, think of the bezel as a clock. First push at 12 o'clock, then on the opposite side at 6 o'clock. Follow by pushing at 3 and at 9 o'clock and then in-between each o'clock until the bezel has been equally pushed at all points around the stone.

5 Use the edge of the burnishing tool or bezel pusher to burnish the silver edge of the bezel around the stone.

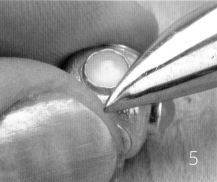

Fine-silver bead cores are designed specifically to fit chains for collectable charm bracelets.

Creating Elaborate Beads

The artichoke bead looks very complex, but it's really just a combination of tiny overlapping pieces of metal clay applied one after the other to complete the bead. Since it takes time to apply each little piece of clay, a slow-drying clay is needed to keep the bead from drying out as you work. This bead is worth the effort, because it receives a lot of attention due to the visual and textural intricacy of its form.

MATERIALS YOU'LL NEED FOR AN
ARTICHOKE BEAD:
Art Clay Silver Slow-Dry
Basic metal clay tools
    (see pages 16–18)
⅜-inch (10mm) teardrop-shaped cutter
    (Kemper Klay Kutters work well)
Cork clay
Chain for hanging

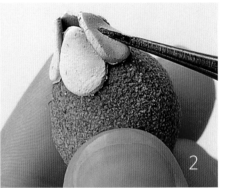

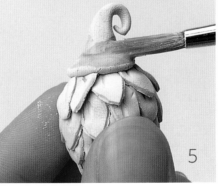

1 Make a cork clay bead core in the shape of a teardrop. Let the cork clay dry. Roll out a sheet of metal clay about three playing cards thick. Cut out flat teardrop shapes with the teardrop-shaped cutter. Cut out as many as you can fit from the sheet of clay. Keep the clay covered with plastic wrap to keep moist.

2 Start at the pointed end of the cork clay bead core. Apply the teardrop shapes next to one another, slightly overlapping with the pointed ends toward the point of the core form. Use water to attach the pieces. Make a vertical mark in the center of each teardrop shape with a needle tool.

3 Continue adding teardrop shapes in rows, each overlapping the last.

4 Finish covering the core with a round pad of clay on the top of the bead.

5 Make the stem of the bead with a tapered piece of fresh, moist clay. Quickly coil the tapered end of the clay into a loop before the clay starts to dry. Attach the thick end of the stem piece with slip to the top of the bead. Decorate the pointed end with a small ball. Fire the bead on a fiber blanket in a kiln (Art Clay Silver Slow-Dry = 1472°F [244°C] for thirty minutes). Finish the bead with a brass scratch brush and hang it on a chain.

Beads | 73

Beads

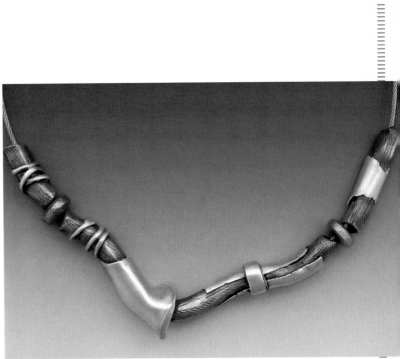

left: *Silver Artichoke Bead* by Sherri Haab.

top right: *Branches* by Hadar Jacobson. Copper and silver metal clays. Photo by the artist.

above: *Group of PMC Beads* by Barbara Becker Simon. Fine silver. Photo by Larry Sanders.

bottom right: *Little Fish Bead* by Barbara Becker Simon. Fine silver, synthetic spinel, and hollow. Photo by Rob Stegmann.

setting stones

One unique feature about metal clay is the ability to set stones directly into the clay and then fire them in place, which is a quick alternative to the traditional method of setting stones in metal. Cubic zirconia and some synthetic (lab-grown) stones, such as rubies and sapphires, are a few stones that will withstand high-firing temperatures. In addition, several metal clay suppliers sell a variety of stones that can be fired successfully with metal clay. If you use a synthetic stone, make sure it is not a "simulate," which means the stone can be made out of anything that resembles the stone (including glass) and may not be able to withstand heat.

Stones such as moonstone, hematite, garnet, and peridot can be fired with low-firing metal clays. Fire these stones at the lowest temperature possible and use either PMC3, fired at 1110°F (599°C), or Art Clay Silver 650, fired at 1200°F (649°C). Soft stones, including turquoise, opals, and pearls, need to be set after firing the metal clay.

Care should be taken when firing stones into gold metal clay due to its high firing temperature and lengthy firing time. Cubic zirconia and corundums (rubies and sapphires) can be successfully fired into gold clay. The quality of a stone must also be taken into consideration, as a stone's imperfections are vulnerable at its stress points, which might fracture during firing. You can also set stones in projects that combine gold and silver metal clays. Prefire the gold clay portion first, and then add a low-fire silver clay with stones.

To fire a stone in place, surround the stone with a bezel that will shrink around it. Make sure that the bezel is higher than the girdle of the stone so that the stone does not pop over the rim. Let fired stones cool slowly to prevent the stones from shattering or clouding. It helps to keep the kiln door shut to ensure gradual cooling. The projects in this section show different methods for setting stones both before and after firing. Experiment and use whichever method you prefer.

FIRING GEMSTONES IN METAL CLAY

Some gemstones can be set into metal clay and fired in place. The following two charts were created as a guideline for firing stones. The information is based on kiln and torch tests performed initially by Kevin Whitmore of Rio Grande and then further tested and compiled by Mardel Rein.

Since natural gemstones contain imperfections, some may not survive firing, even though the chart includes them—or your own attempts to fire the same stone proved to be successful.

The chart is only a guide to help artists in gauging which stones have been previously tested and which have a greater chance of survival.

This chart classifies stones as No Fire, Low Fire, and High Fire. High fire stones are those that can withstand 1650°F (899°C) for at least one hour with no color change. No fire stones are those that must be set after firing. Low fire stones are those that are heat sensitive with a risk of color change.

Natural Gemstone Firing Chart
Maximum Suggested Firing Temp/Time (Kiln set at full ramp speed)

GEMSTONE	MINERAL GROUP	NO FIRE	LOW FIRE	HIGH FIRE	TORCH
Agate (Cameo)	Quartz	X			
Alexandrite [1]	Chrysoberyl			1650°F (899°C)/1H	X
Alexandrite Cat's Eye [1]	Chrysoberyl			1650°F (899°C)/2H	
Almandine	Garnet		1560°F (849°C)/30M		X
Amazonite	Feldspar		1200°F (649°C)/30M		
Aquamarine	Beryl	X			
Aventurine	Quartz	X			
Black Onyx	Quartz	X			
Black Star Sapphire	Corundum			1650°F (899°C)/2H	X
Carnelian	Quartz	X			
Chalcedony	Quartz	X			
Chrome diopside	Pyroxene		1200°F (649°C)/30M		
Citrine	Quartz	X			
Demantoid	Garnet		1560°F (849°C)/30M		X
Denim lapis	Rock	X			
Diamond [2]	Diamond	X			
Emerald	Beryl	X			
Fire Opal	Silicate	X			
Green Tourmaline	Tourmaline			1200°F (649°C)/30M	
Hematite	Iron Mineral			1650°F (899°C)/2H	X
Iolite	Iolite	X			
Jadeite	Pyroxene	X			
Labradorite	Feldspar		1200°F (649°C)/30M		

GEMSTONE	MINERAL GROUP	NO FIRE	LOW FIRE	HIGH FIRE	TORCH
Lapis lazuli [3]	Rock	X			
Malachite	Borate	X			
Moonstone—Gray	Feldspar		1200°F (649°C)/30M		
Moonstone—Peach	Feldspar		1110°F (599°C)/30M		
Moonstone—White	Feldspar		1110°F (599°C)/30M		
Padparadscha	Corundum			1650°F (899°C)/2H	X
Peridot	Olivine			1470°F (799°C)/30M	X
Pink Tourmaline	Tourmaline	X			
Pyrite [4]	Sulphide	X			
Pyrope	Garnet		1560°F (849°C)/30M		X
Rhodocrosite	Calcite	X			
Rhodolite	Garnet		1470°F (799°C)/30M		X
Rose Quartz	Quartz	X			
Ruby	Corundum			1650°F (899°C)/2H	X
Rutiliated Quartz	Quartz	X			
Sapphire	Corundum			1650°F (899°C)/2H	X
Smokey Quartz	Quartz	X			
Spinel	Spinel			1650°F (899°C)/1H	
Star diopside	Pyroxene		1200°F (649°C)/30M		
Sunstone	Feldspar		1200°F (649°C)/30M		
Tanzanite	Zoisite			1600°F (871°C)/30	X
Topaz (all varieties)	Topaz	X			
Tsavorite	Garnet		1470°F (799°C)/30M		X
Turquoise [5]	Phosphate	X			
Zircon	Nesosilicate			1650°F (899°C)/1H	X

1 Some believe this stone is either too hard to find or is too expensive to use. It can be pricey, but there are plenty of sources for this stone, including Cat's Eye. Loupe the stone before firing. Do not fire if you see bubbles.

2 Diamonds are risky in the kiln. There have been a few firing successes for diamonds. If you do fire, keep your time and temperature low. Diamonds can take a lot of heat, but not for long. Since results are both inconsistent and inconclusive, it is probably better to set diamonds after firing or wait until further testing indicates a safe method for firing diamonds.

3 Lapis lazuli is not a mineral, but a microcrystaline rock composed mainly of the mineral lazurite, with some pyrite and white calcite. Denim lapis is a low-quality lapis with less lazurite and more white calcite.

4 Pyrite is dangerous in the kiln. Pyrite contains sulphur, which can be explosive when heated.

5 Turquoise is a secondary mineral of hydrated copper aluminum phosphate.

This chart was adapted from a firing chart created by Mardel Rein. Used by permission ©2005–2007 by Mardel Rein / Distributed by Cool Tools. www.cooltools.us

Cubic Zirconia and Lab Gemstone Firing Chart
Maximum Suggested Firing Temp/Time (Kiln set at full ramp speed)

GEMSTONE	MINERAL GROUP	NO FIRE	LOW FIRE	HIGH FIRE	TORCH
CZ Amethyst	Simulant			1650°F (899°C)/2H	X
CZ Champagne	Simulant			1650°F (899°C)/2H	X
CZ Emerald (bright) [1]	Simulant		1110°F (599°C)/10M		
CZ Garnet	Simulant			1650°F (899°C)/2H	X
CZ Light Amethyst	Simulant			1650°F (899°C)/2H	X
CZ Olivine (dark) [2]	Simulant			1650°F (899°C)/1H	X
CZ Orange [3]	Simulant		1560°F (849°C)/20M		X
CZ Pink	Simulant			1650°F (899°C)/2H	X
CZ Tanzanite [4]	Simulant		1110°F (599°C)/10M		
CZ White	Simulant			1650°F (899°C)/2H	X
CZ Yellow	Simulant			1650°F (899°C)/2H	X
Lab Alexandrite	Synthetic			1650°F (899°C)/2H	X
Lab Emerald [5]	Synthetic		1470°F (799°C)/30M		
Lab Opal	Synthetic	X			
Lab Ruby	Synthetic			1650°F (899°C)/2H	X
Lab Sapphire Blue	Synthetic			1650°F (899°C)/2H	X
Lab Sapphire Orange [6]	Synthetic			1650°F (899°C)/1H	X
Lab Sapphire Yellow [7]	Synthetic			1650°F (899°C)/1H	X
Lab Spinel	Synthetic			1650°F (899°C)/2H	X

1 All bright green CZs are extremely heat sensitive. Fire at 1110°F (599°C) for ten minutes for any bright green stone, regardless of color name.

2 CZs in an olive hue are stable up to 1650°F (899°C) for one hour.

3 Orange CZs can be fired up to two hours at 1650°F (899°C), but color will fade.

4 Tanzanite CZs incur a very slight darkening, but no color loss at 1110°F (599°C) for ten minutes. Do not extend time. Extremely heat sensitive.

5 Temperature given is for hydrothermal grown gems.

6 This stone can darken after two hours at 1650°F (899°C). The color will become a bit more orange and intense.

7 This stone can darken after two hours at 1650°F (899°C). The color will become a bit more orange and intense.

Firing with Stones

These pins were made using stones that can be fired in place. The stones were set easily into wet metal clay using a rope of clay as a bezel for each. The Christmas tree and butterfly pins were created using the same stone-setting technique. Slight variations in technique and supplies for each are noted in the following instructions.

MATERIALS YOU'LL NEED FOR PINS:
Art Clay Silver
Art Clay Silver Syringe Type
Basic metal clay tools (*see pages 16–18*)
Colored cubic zirconia stones (*various colors and shapes*)
.950 silver pin back

ADDITIONAL MATERIALS FOR
A CHRISTMAS TREE PIN:
Shade-Tex® rubbing plates (*see Resources*)

1 To make a Christmas tree pin, roll out a thick sheet of metal clay about five playing cards thick. Roll a texture onto the surface of the clay with a Shade-Tex rubbing plate. Oil the sheet to prevent sticking.

2 Cut out a Christmas tree shape with a knife.

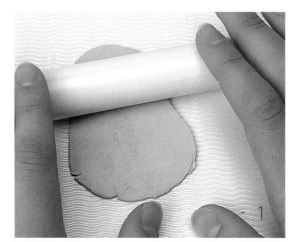

3 Press cubic zirconia stones onto the clay surface. Use syringe metal clay to surround each stone with a rope of clay. Dry the pin until it is bone-dry. The bezels around the stones can be smoothed with water and a paintbrush as the pin dries.

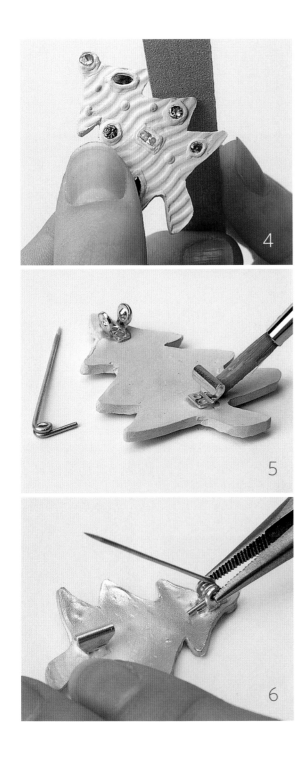

4 Sand the edges of the dried pin with a nail file until smooth.

5 Measure the placement of the pin back. Cut the pin portion of the finding to the proper length, if necessary, and file to a point. Use thick slip to attach the catch and the hinge of the pin back. Do not attach the pin part until after firing. Apply several layers of thick slip for a secure bond. Fire the pin on a kiln shelf (Art Clay Silver = 1472°F [800°C] for thirty minutes). Finish the pin with a brass scratch brush. Burnish the raised area of the texture with a burnishing tool.

6 Slide the pin into the hinge part of the pin back. Pinch the hinge shut with pliers. As an alternative to the above step, you could glue a pin back onto the clay pin with epoxy.

This piece is reminiscent of vintage rhinestone pins that are popular collectibles today.

Brass stamping of butterfly

1 To make a butterfly pin, roll out a thick sheet of metal clay about six to seven playing cards thick. Press the brass stamping into the clay to transfer its texture.

2 Cut out the butterfly shape with a knife.

3 An alternative method: Make a mold of the stamping with a two-part silicone mold compound (see pages 56–57).

4 Follow the instructions in steps 3–6 of the Christmas tree pin project to finish.

Silver Metal Clay and colored CZ
stones fired in place by Sherri Haab.
Photo by Dan Haab.

Making Bezels for Delicate Stones

For stones that cannot withstand the firing process, you can make a fine-silver wire bezel to set into the clay before firing, which will also ensure that the bezel will fit the stone after firing. The stone is set after the piece is fired and finished. These clever, fine-silver bezel wires are made especially for metal clay, and can be fired in place with the help of tabs that embed into the clay.

MATERIALS YOU'LL NEED FOR A PENDANT:

PMC3 or Art Clay Silver 650

Basic metal clay tools (*see pages 16–18*)

Fine–silver-tabbed bezel wire
(*available from Metal Clay Findings, see Resources*)

Permanent pen

Wire cutters

Stone to set after firing (*Drusy Quartz was used in this project*)

Leather stamping tool, or other texturing tool

Fine-silver balls (*available from Metal Clay Findings, see Resources*)

Silverware handle, or other object to make texture for the bail

Drinking straw

Bezel pusher, or burnishing tool

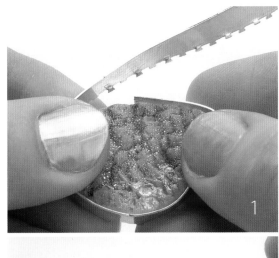

1 Choose a fine–silver-tabbed bezel wire that is a bit taller than the height of your stone. A bezel wire contains tabs with every other tab bent at a 90-degree angle, which will serve as the seat for the stone. The other tabs will embed into the clay to make a mechanical connection. Wrap the bezel wire around the outside edge of the stone to form the bezel. Don't wrap the stone too tightly; leave a bit of wiggle room around it. Make sure that the bent tabs face inward toward the stone.

2 With a permanent pen, mark the bezel wire at the point where the wire completely surrounds the stone.

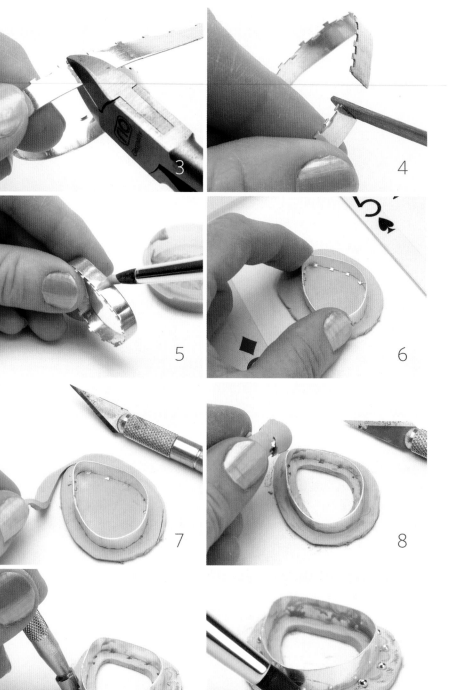

3 With wire cutters, cut the bezel wire as straight and square as possible at the pen mark.

4 Use a small file to clean up the cut edge if needed. Be careful not to remove too much material, or the bezel will be too small. To close the gap at the seam, overlap the ends of the wire pulling one past the other. Align the edges to meet; the gap should stay closed due to spring tension.

5 Make sure the bezel wire still fits around the stone, shaping it as needed. Use a clay tool or brush to apply thick slip over the seam on both the outside and inside of the bezel. Gently refine the slip as it dries, being careful not to disturb or chip it off prior to firing. Fire the bezel for five to ten minutes at 1650°F (899°C).

6 After firing and cooling the bezel, roll out a sheet of clay about five playing cards thick. Press the bezel into the clay. The straight tabs of the bezel wire will embed into the clay layer. The bent tabs will appear on top of the clay sheet inside the bezel.

7 Trim the clay around the edge of the bezel, leaving a border to decorate.

8 Cut the clay from the middle of the bezel, leaving a small border to conceal the tabs.

9 Use a leather stamping tool or other object to texture the clay around the edge of the bezel.

10 To add silver balls to decorate the bezel, make depressions into the clay with the tip of a clay shaper tool. Add slip to each depression and

push the silver balls into the slip using the chisel end of the shaper tool. Push the balls about halfway into the clay.

11 Use a paintbrush with water or slip to refine the clay edges both inside and outside of the bezel.

12 To make the bail (the tube to hang the pendant) for the top of the bezel, roll out a sheet of clay, about three playing cards thick, into a strip and texture it with a piece of silverware or other texture tool.

13 Trim the edges of the strip of clay to a desired width and quickly wrap it around a drinking straw to form the bail. Cut the strip to fit loosely around the straw and blend the seam with a clay shaper tool.

14 Sand and score the top of the bail to provide a surface area to attach the bail. Let both pieces dry until they are leather-hard. Remove the bail from the straw prior to attaching it to the bezel.

15 Attach the bail to the top of the bezel with slip. On the back of the bezel, add a small strip of clay over the seam for extra security. Smooth with more slip or water using a brush.

16 Fire the bezel in a kiln as directed for PMC3 or Art Clay Silver 650. After firing, finish the clay metal by burnishing and applying a patina.

17 Remove the patina from the raised texture with a polishing pad.

18 Push the stone into the bezel.

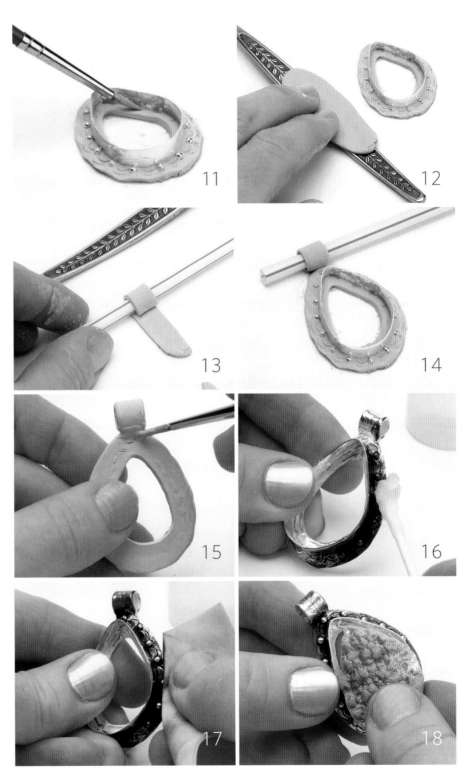

19 Use a bezel pusher or burnishing tool to press the top edge of the bezel wire in and around the top of the stone. Push the wire on opposite sides and on the top and bottom. Then continue to push around the entire edge to set the stone. Think of the bezel as if it were a clock face. Push at twelve o'clock and six o'clock, and then at three o'clock and nine o'clock. Afterward, push the rest of the bezel edge.

19

The completed setting displayed on a strand of Labradorite beads.

Setting Pearls

Floral earrings made with PMC3 silver clay make a quick and easy gift. These drop earrings require very little clay. In addition, everything is assembled prior to firing, with no need to solder. The earrings' color can even be personalized for the recipient. Pearls are available in a variety of colors, from rich purples and brown tones to light pastel shades of ivory, peach, and gray.

MATERIALS YOU'LL NEED FOR PEARL FLORAL EARRINGS:

PMC3

Basic metal clay tools (*see pages 16–18*)

¼- (6mm) and ⅜-inch (10mm) teardrop-shaped cutters (*Kemper Klay Kutters work well*)

Fine .999 silver wire

Two half-drilled pearls

Two sterling silver ear wires

Two-part epoxy

Patina (*optional*)

1 Roll out a thin sheet of metal clay about three playing cards thick. Cut out five ⅜-inch (10mm) teardrop shapes with the cutter to make the petals. Make one earring at a time so that the clay will not dry out. Keep the clay covered with plastic wrap to keep moist.

2 Make a small ball of clay for the center of the flower. Press the petals onto the clay center, overlapping one over the other. Use water to attach the petals to the center and to each other. Work quickly to keep the petals from drying out.

3 Cut out five ¼-inch (6mm) teardrop shapes with the cutter to make the leaves. Score veins on each leaf and attach the five leaves to the base of the flower. Overlap each one slightly and adhere with water. Add more water or slip to secure the petals and leaves.

4 Roll a clay snake and make a small loop to attach to the base of each flower earring. Use slip and water to attach, smoothing with a brush.

5 Turn each earring over, and insert a fine .999 silver wire into the center of each flower. Add slip around the wire to keep it in place. Let the flowers set until bone-dry. Fire the earrings on a bed of fiber blanket (PMC3=1650°F [899°C] for five minutes). Finish the earrings with a brass scratch brush. After brushing, it's a good idea to tumble the earrings to work-harden the fine-silver wires (see page 42). (Jewelry makers routinely work-harden metal by burnishing, hammering, pulling wire, or tumbling. In this case, the tumbler does the burnishing.)

6 Dip the finished earrings into a patina solution if desired. Buff with a polishing cloth to remove the patina from the raised areas. Check the fit of the pearls, and clip the wires if too long. Glue the pearls onto the wires at the center of each earring with two-part epoxy.

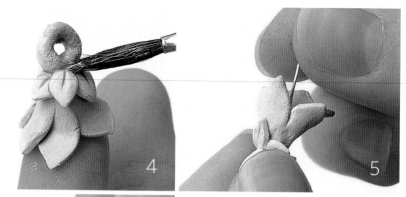

To complete the project, use pliers to attach a sterling silver ear wire to the loop of each earring.

Stone-Setting

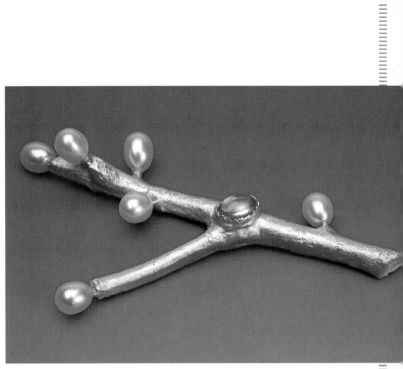

above: *Moonstone Pendant* by Jennifer Kahn. Fine silver, moonstone, and sterling silver. Photo by the artist.

top right: *Silver Twig* by Sherri Haab. Fine silver, half-drilled pearls, and sterling silver. Photo by Dan Haab.

bottom right: *Arbol de Vida* by Lorena Angulo. Hand-sculpted and carved PMC3 with cubic zirconia garnet. Photo by George Post.

rings

Rings are great to make with metal clay for several reasons. One is that only a small amount of clay is needed to make a finished ring; another is that the clay allows you a lot of artistic freedom in the design. Rings, however, require more attention to forming and craftsmanship than other metal clay projects. You will need to take into account the fit and design of the ring as you work, since metal clay shrinks in the firing process and different clay types have different shrinkage rates. There are ways to calculate the finished ring size and also accessories that aid in controlling the shrinkage and shape of the ring during the firing process.

Your design will also affect the strength and integrity of the finished ring. The strength of a finished ring is dependent on two factors: (1) using the right clay, and (2) making a design that is structurally sound without thin or weak areas that are vulnerable to bending or breaking. Tumbling the finished ring in stainless steel shot also helps to strengthen a ring because it work-hardens the metal.

PMC3 or Art Clay Silver Slow-Dry clays are good to use for making rings. Using Slow-Dry clay prevents the ring from drying out and cracking as you form it around a ring mandrel, a rod used by jewelers to shape and size rings. Bronze and copper clay can also be used to make rings in the same fashion as silver and gold. Make sure you follow the firing instructions for these types of clays. Having the right tools, such as mandrels, firing accessories, and measuring tools, is helpful in making successful finished rings.

Rustic Rings by Jennifer Kahn. Fine silver, carved conch shell, old coin, and wood bead. Photo by Robert Diamante.

Creating a Simple Ring

An ancient intaglio was molded to make the centerpiece for this simple ring. You could mold a favorite button, old coin, or other found object as the focal point for this antique style ring. The ring shank is fashioned in a half-round wire style for comfort and simplicity. By firing the ring on a form, you can ensure that it will shrink to the right size.

MATERIALS YOU'LL NEED FOR AN
ANTIQUE STYLE RING:

PMC3 or Art Clay 650 Slow-Dry

Basic metal clay tools *(see pages 16–18)*

MultiMandrel

Teflon paper, or HattieS Patties
    ring-forming strip

Cellophane tape

Mat cutter blade, or tissue blade

Mold for clay centerpiece

Oil-based slip

HattieS Patties ring forms

Fiber blanket *(for propping the ring
    during firing)*

Patina *(Black Max)*

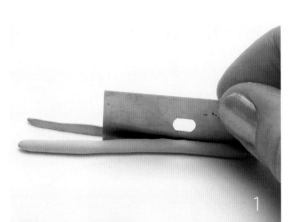

1 Prior to forming the ring, prepare a mandrel that is two sizes larger than the desired size of the finished ring by wrapping it with Teflon or other nonstick paper. (For example, if you want your finished ring to be a size 5, use a size 7 mandrel.) Secure the paper strip with a small piece of cellophane tape to hold. Set the mandrel aside as you form the ring. Begin forming a ring shank by rolling a clay snake. Then cut it in half lengthwise to form a half-round shank.

2 Wrap the clay snake around the prepared mandrel. If the clay overlaps, cut through all the layers at an angle to make a join, or simply blend the ends where they meet.

3 Use a clay shaper tool and water to blend the seam. Blend the clay ends well to join.

4 The shank can dry on the mandrel as you prepare the decorative piece that will be placed in the center of the ring, or you can prepare the piece in advance and let it dry so it will be easier to handle. To make a decorative element to add to the ring, mold a piece of clay using the method for Simple Molds on pages 57–58. After the molded piece has dried, clean up the edges and file or score the back of the piece to roughen it up prior to attaching it to the ring.

5 Use thick oil-based slip to attach the dried decorative piece over the seam of the ring on the mandrel. Apply the slip over the seam of the ring.

6 Press the molded piece over the slip to attach it to the ring.

7 After the ring dries enough to handle, carefully remove it from the mandrel and remove the paper from the center of the ring. Let the ring continue to dry completely. Add more slip to attach a thin strip of clay to the backside of the centerpiece, securing it to the inside seam of the ring. This will give the piece extra strength and make it one solid piece. Add more layers as the piece dries, smoothing each with a paintbrush and water to refine the seams.

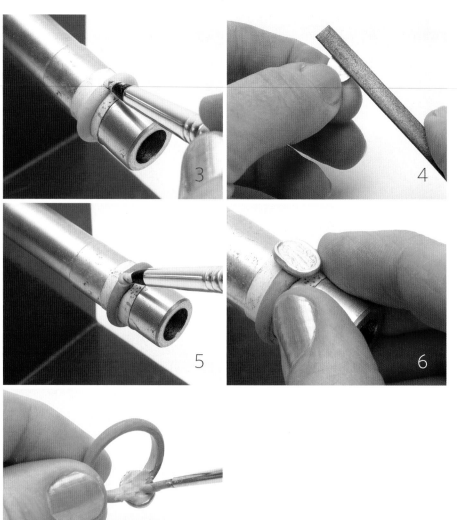

8 Carefully sand the ring, if needed, with fine-sanding or polishing cloths, prior to firing. Place the ring over a ring form in the finished size (two sizes smaller than the mandrel you used to form the ring). Use a fiber blanket to keep the ring level and centered over the form. Fire the ring at the highest temperature recommended for the type of clay you are using for maximum strength.

9 After firing and cooling the ring, the ring form will crumble out of the ring easily, or it may stay intact as you twist it out of the center. Clean the ring and tumble or burnish as desired. For a matte finish, finish with a brass scratch brush. To add sparkle to the centerpiece, burnish select areas by hand, using a stainless steel burnishing tool.

10 To darken the recessed areas, apply patina using a cotton swab.

11 After the patina dries, polish off with a buffing pad.

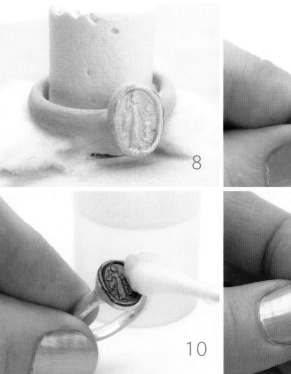

This clay centerpiece was molded from an ancient intaglio. Black Max patina solution was used to bring out the details of the ring.

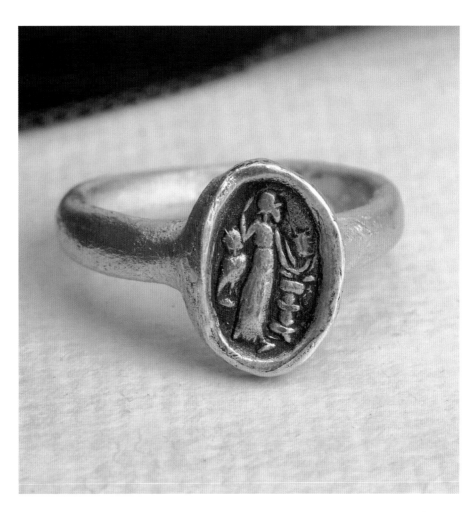

Making a Ring Bezel for Stones

Cut stones add sparkle to a ring. With the ability to fire stones in metal clay, you can take advantage of a variety of unique bezel and setting designs. The idea is simply to surround the stone with clay to hold it in place. Be sure to choose stones that can be fired at high temperatures.

MATERIALS YOU'LL NEED FOR A
STONE RING:
Art Clay Silver Slow-Dry
Basic metal clay tools *(see pages 16–18)*
Teflon paper, or HattieS Patties ring-
    forming strip
Cellophane tape
One 6mm cubic zirconia stone
Ring mandrel
Mallet

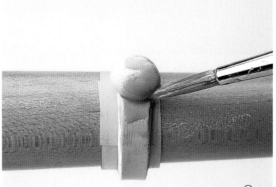

1 Wrap a strip of nonstick paper around a ring mandrel at a place on the mandrel that is two sizes larger than your desired finished size. Secure the paper with a small piece of cellophane tape. Make a band ring by rolling out a sheet of clay that is five playing cards thick. Cut a strip in your desired width to form the ring band and wrap it around the mandrel. Cut through the overlapped layers of clay at an angle as shown. Remove the excess clay. Join the seam with a clay shaper tool to blend the clay ends together.

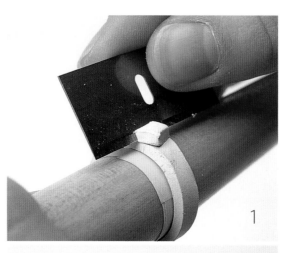

2 After you have joined the band at the seam, attach a ball of clay over the seam with slip and water.

3 Push a cubic zirconia stone into the ball of clay until the girdle of the stone is just below the surface of the clay. Add more slip at the attachment and fix

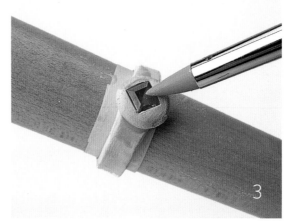

imperfections as the ring dries, if needed. Let the ring dry until bone-dry. Fire the ring by kiln or torch. Remember to cool a ring containing a stone slowly. To be extra safe, leave the kiln door shut until cool, or air-cool if using a torch.

Birthstone rings are a fun project to make, and there are a variety of colorful lab-grown stones from which to choose.

Rings

left: *Mamma, Did You Sing?* by Donna Penoyer. Bird whistle ring. Photo by the artist.

above: *Organic Ring* by Lorena Angulo. Fine-silver band wrapped with PMC3. Photo by the artist.

bronze &
copper clays

Bronze and copper clays are nonprecious metal clays that can be sculpted, textured, and shaped like silver and gold clays. In many ways all metal clays are similar, consisting of powder metal particles combined with organic binder and water. Although the particles for bronze and copper sinter similarly to silver metal clay during firing, a few variables must be taken into account to properly fire bronze and copper clays. One of the best qualities of these metal clays is that they are less expensive than precious metal clays, which allows you the freedom to make larger pieces and experiment without a big financial commitment.

Bronze clay consists of copper and tin particles suspended in an organic binder, which creates a solid bronze object after the binder burns away and the particles sinter during firing. Copper clay consists of pure copper particles mixed with an organic binder. Both types of clays shrink about twenty to twenty-five percent; however, their shrinkage rate is not always proportional. For example, some shapes shrink more in thickness than in length. Both clays are smooth and pliable, and can be sculpted, rolled, textured, and carved to make a variety of projects.

Fired bronze and copper clays can be finished in the same manner as silver metal clay. A piece can be left as is or burnished to bring out the bright gold color of the bronze. Use a stainless steel scratch brush for copper if you want to avoid turning the copper into a gold color. Bronze has a warm gold color, with a variety of options for finishes. Fired copper ranges from rustic red to rich brown hues.

Both clays are very strong and dense when fired properly, which is perfect for jewelry pieces such as cuff-style bracelets that require strength for the integrity of the piece. Copper and bronze clay can also be combined to make mixed-media pieces by firing the copper clay first and then adding the bronze clay to the fired copper. The clay piece is then fired a second time at the bronze clay's firing temperature, resulting in stunning combinations of gold- and copper-colored pieces. Silver may also be introduced and fired in combination with copper, or it can be fired with bronze under certain conditions (see page 35).

Bronze or Copper Clay Beads

Copper and bronze clays present a bit of a challenge when it comes to bead making. Earlier methods and formulations needed for firing situations will not work well for hollow forms. With new methods and clay variations it is now possible to form beads over combustible forms and then fire them similarly to silver clay methods. Bronze and copper shrink quite a bit, so try to keep the clay loosely wrapped over bead cores to avoid splitting. Tube beads are easy to form, but pay particular attention when joining seams. Other shapes are made using bead cores that are then fired in place.

Tube Beads

To make tube beads, a straw or similar item can be used to form the beads. These beads can be fired using either firing schedule for bronze or copper clay.

MATERIALS YOU'LL NEED FOR TUBE BEADS:

Bronze metal clay

Basic metal clay tools (see pages 16–18)

Textures to pattern the beads, such as patterned silverware

Plastic straw

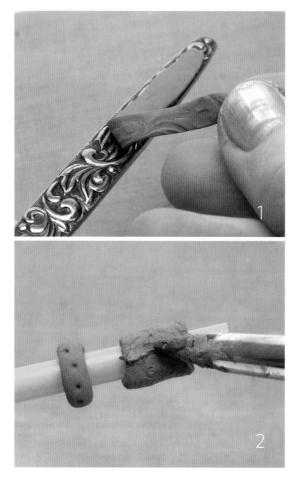

1 Roll out a clay snake and flatten it onto a texture, such as the handle of a piece of silverware.

2 Quickly wrap a strip of clay loosely around a plastic straw, overlapping the clay and cutting through both thicknesses. Or you can leave the clay overlapping intentionally for the design. Blend the seam with a clay shaper tool; add oil-based paste or thick slip, and continue to blend the seam well.

3 As the tube bead dries, fill in the seam and add fresh clay to make sure the join is secure. Smooth the seam with water and a brush, adding the texture again if needed.

4 After a few hours, slide the bead off the straw to finish drying. Add more clay to the inside seam and to the outside to keep the bead from splitting. After the beads are dry, sand the edges using sanding papers or an emery board to finish. Fire the beads in carbon as directed for bronze clay. Finish the beads by burnishing them or adding a patina after the beads are cooled. If a tube bead splits after firing, you can repair it by adding more clay to fill the seam and then refiring it.

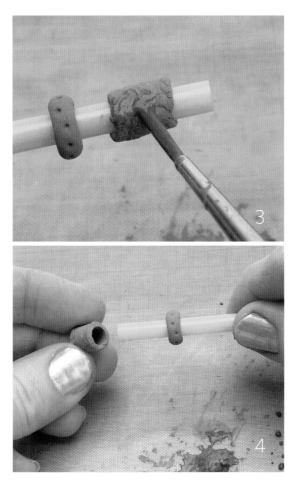

Bronze tube beads over sterling silver Viking knit bracelet by Sherri Haab. Photo by the artist.

Beads over Cores

Form dimensional beads over bead cores, which will either burn away or remain in place after firing, depending on the material you use for the core. Keep the metal clay wrapped loosely around the core to prevent splitting as the bead fires.

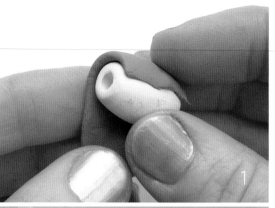

MATERIALS YOU'LL NEED FOR
BEADS OVER CORES:

Bronze metal clay

Basic metal clay tools *(see pages 16–18)*

Sobo, or PVA white glue

Paperclay, bisque ceramic bead, or cork clay *(If using Paperclay, form a shape by hand and let it dry; if using cork clay for bead cores, apply the two-stage firing schedule for bronze clay found on page 34.)*

Leather stamping tool, or other texturing tool

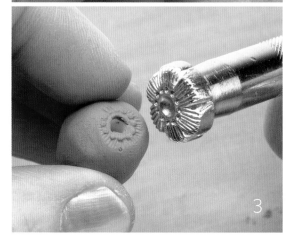

1 Coat the bead core first with a layer of glue and let it dry. Roll out a sheet of clay about three playing cards thick to cover the bead core. Wrap the clay loosely around the bead core, as the clay will shrink during the firing process.

2 Trim the clay to fit the bead core and blend the seam with a clay shaper tool. Add paste or slip and smooth seams and repair cracks in the bead.

3 Stamp designs on the end of the clay bead with a leather stamping tool or other texturing tool. Create pilot holes with a needle tool to string on each end of the bead if you are using paper

clay. If you are using a bisque ceramic bead, use a needle tool to pierce the clay through the existing hole. Refine the holes when the clay is dry with the tip of a knife (see page 26).

4 Decorate the clay bead with textured clay. Attach the clay using paste or slip.

5 Add details and secure with a clay shaper tool. As the clay dries, repair cracks or splits with fresh clay.

6 After the clay beads are dry, fire them as directed for bronze clay, using the appropriate schedule for the bead core. If the clay bead has splits after firing, fill the gaps with fresh clay, blending well. Dry and refire the clay beads. After firing, the bisque ceramic bead will remain inside the clay bead. If you wish to remove the Paperclay for a hollow bead, you can chip away the clay inside the bead using a needle tool and then soaking it in water until cleaned. Combustible types of cores will burn away during firing.

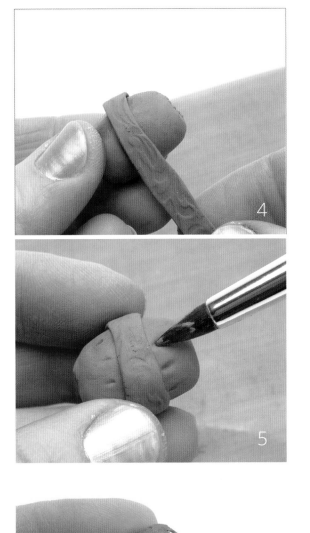

Some richly textured bronze clay beads by Sherri Haab.

Creating Links

Copper clay is fairly flexible in the leather-hard stage, so it is easy to cut and link dry pieces together. Bronze clay also allows you to flex the links open to attach pieces prior to firing. Silver links can be made similarly; however, the links may break using the same technique. Instead, build silver links around each other in stages, piecing dry parts together using slip or wet clay.

MATERIALS YOU'LL NEED
FOR A LINK BRACELET:

Copper metal clay

Copper clay slip or paste

Basic metal clay tools (*see pages 16–18*)

Texture sheets

Leather stamping tool, or other
    texturing tool

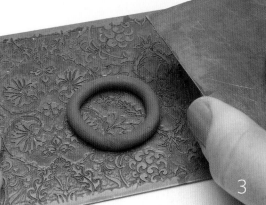

1 This bracelet consists of two types of links: large textured links alternated with smaller plain links. Make the links one at a time so that the clay will not dry out as you work. Roll out a clay snake to make the first large textured links.

2 Quickly form the clay snake into a circle, overlapping the ends. Blend the ends with your fingers.

3 Place the clay circle onto a textured sheet.

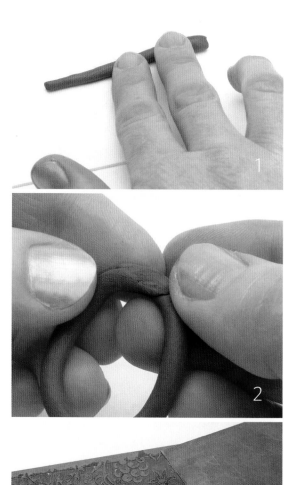

4   Press another textured sheet over the clay circle and apply pressure to flatten it. This will give texture to both sides of the link.

5   Lift the textured link from the sheet.

6   Continue to form the remaining large links in the same fashion. Afterward, make smaller links by forming thin clay snakes into oval shapes. These smaller links will connect the large links.

7   Make a toggle by forming a strip of clay that is two-and-a-half times the length in diameter of the open space of the first link. This will serve as the clasp. Texture both sides of the toggle. Make a small loop on one side of the toggle and attach it, blending with paste and clay. Let the toggle dry for a few hours. Let the links dry for a few hours, or until the clay is dry enough to handle without distorting the clay.

8   To prepare the pieces to link together, make one cut through each large textured link.

9   Gently pull open the link where the cut was made. Pull sideways, not apart, which would cause more stress.

10   Add two small oval links to the large link. (This photo shows one of the links being added.)

11   Apply slip or paste to the join.

12 Press the ends of the clay together. Hold the piece and apply pressure for about a minute to ensure the join is adhered.

13 Apply paste over the seam. This will serve both to cover the join's seam and to allow for a decorative element, which will add strength to the join.

14 Apply a piece of clay to cover both sides of the seam.

15 Smooth the clay over the seam of the join and add texture with a leather stamping tool, or other texturing tool.

16 Continue to add links to form the length of the bracelet. Add a few simple links at the end of the bracelet where the toggle will be added. Copper links tend to shrink more in thickness than in length. Make the bracelet about ½ to 1 inch (1.3 to 2.5cm) longer than the finished length should be.

17 Cut and open one of the simple links at the end of the chain and add the toggle. Apply paste and patch over the seam of the cut link with fresh, moist clay for extra security. Smooth the link as it dries with a brush and water. Dry the entire piece for several days to ensure that the clay is free of moisture before firing.

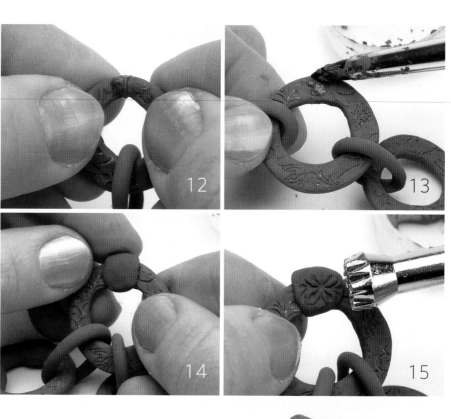

18 To fire the bracelet, position the links close together on a layer of carbon. Place the large links close together, which will allow room for the smaller links to shrink in and around the large links. Form the bracelet into a circle as needed to fit into the pan. Keep the links at least ½ inch (1.3cm) from the sides of the pan. Cover the bracelet with a layer of carbon and fire according to the copper clay's firing schedule (see page 39). After cooling, finish the clay piece as desired. Burnish with a brass or stainless steel scratch brush, or tumble for a brighter finish. Add a patina if you would like to emphasize the texture.

Copper clay is flexible, making it the perfect medium for sturdy link bracelets.

Combining Copper and Bronze Clays

If you want to make a mixed-metal clay piece, use copper clay as the foundation, firing it first, and then add the bronze clay and fire again. Refire according to the bronze clay's firing schedule (see page 38) for the second firing. Bronze clay sinters at a lower temperature than copper clay, so always fire the copper clay piece first before adding bronze.

This cuff bracelet was created by forming a foundation rope, which was then embellished with a second layer of textured clay. You can make the bracelet using one type of clay by adding the decorative layer after air-drying the foundation. Or, if you want to make a mixed-metal clay piece, use copper clay as the foundation, firing it first and then adding the bronze clay and firing again. Refire according to the bronze clay's firing schedule for the second firing. Bronze clay sinters at a lower temperature than copper clay, so always fire the copper clay piece first before adding bronze.

MATERIALS YOU'LL NEED
FOR A CUFF BRACELET:

Copper or bronze metal clays
Basic metal clay tools (see pages 16–18)
Patterned knife handle, or other
    texturing tool
Bracelet mandrel
One cubic zirconia stone
Mallet

Copper and bronze metal clays were used for these bracelets. Photo by Sherri Haab.

1 Roll out a rope of clay that is at least 9 inches (23cm) in length and ⅜ of an inch (10mm) thick to form the cuff bracelet. Cut the rope about 2 inches (5cm) longer in length than the finished cuff will be. (For example, a 7-inch [18cm] bracelet should be cut at 9 inches [23cm] in length.) Curve the rope into an oval bracelet shape, leaving about 1¼ inches (3.2cm) of space for the opening. Let the rope dry until leather-hard. Use a nail file to round and neaten the ends. Brush the rope with water to smooth any hairline cracks or imperfections. Let the bracelet dry completely.

2 If you are making a copper clay bracelet to which you will add bronze clay, fire the copper clay first before adding the bronze clay. After firing, do not burnish the copper; simply add the bronze clay and then refire according to the bronze clay's firing schedule (see page 38). If the decorative strip will be made of the same clay, proceed to add it to the dried foundation rope formed in step 1. Roll out another thin strip of clay and texture using the handle of a piece of silverware or other texturing tool.

3 Add a layer of paste or slip to attach the decorative strip around the dried foundation rope. If you are adding bronze clay to a fired copper piece, be careful when applying the paste and avoid getting the bronze color onto the copper—where it is not wanted.

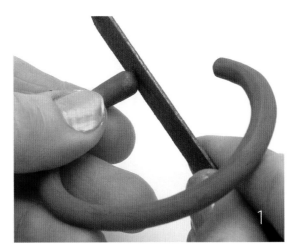

4 Wrap the textured decorative strip around the dried, or fired, foundation rope, adding paste as needed to attach.

5 Add a decorative ball of clay to the center of the cuff with paste. Stamp a design with a leather stamping tool, or other texturing tool.

6 Press a cubic zirconia stone into the center of the textured ball. Embed the stone deep enough to capture the girdle of the stone beneath the surface of the clay.

7 Let the piece dry. Add more paste to repair cracks and to secure attachments.

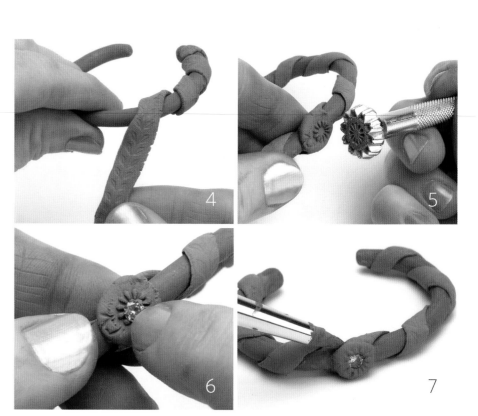

8 After the piece is thoroughly dry, use a file to refine the edges of the clay. If you're making a mixed-metal clay piece, clean the copper portion with a damp cloth or stiff brush with water to remove all residue of the bronze clay from the copper clay prior to firing. Fire the bracelet using the appropriate firing temperature and schedule for the clay you're using. If bronze clay was added to the prefired copper piece, use the bronze clay's firing schedule for the second firing. After firing and cooling the piece, the cuff bracelet will need to be reshaped. Use a mallet to form the metal clay around a bracelet mandrel. If making a mixed-metal piece, shape the copper before adding the bronze, as it will be easier to shape the soft copper to fit your wrist. Burnish the bracelet with a stainless steel scratch brush after the final firing.

9 Add shine to the raised details with a burnishing tool. Add a patina if you would like to darken the metal. Then use a polishing cloth to remove the patina from the raised details.

Bronze & Copper Clays

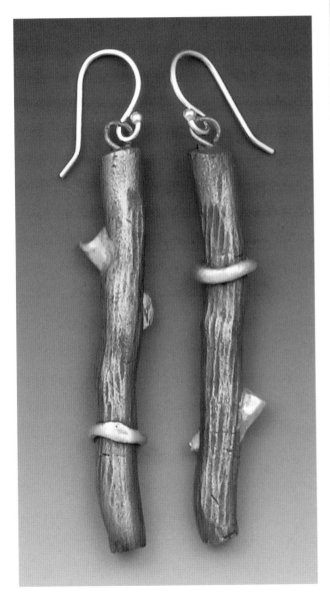

above: *Rose Thorns* by Hadar Jacobson. Copper and silver metal clays. Photo by the artist.

top right: *Corazón Pendant* by Lorena Angulo. Hand-carved heart made with COPPRclay. Photo by the artist.

bottom right: *Bronze Greek Script Pendant* by Christina Leonard. Bronze-carved toggle, bronze rectangular-carved pendant, and bronze dragonfly lentil pendant. Photo by the artist.

gold
metal clay

Gold clay fires to a beautiful, rich yellow-gold color. Because it is a high-karat gold, it is more expensive than silver metal clay. In addition, because gold is a soft metal, it may not be appropriate for pieces that are subject to stress, such as a ring shank. The clay itself is very smooth and easy to work with. Water is used to keep it moist, to attach pieces, or to make slip, like silver clay.

Gold is formulated in a karat that can be fired at similar temperatures to silver clay. Refer to the charts on pages 36 to 37 for more information on firing temperatures. You can use gold clay in combination with silver, or use pure gold for an extra special project.

Since gold is expensive, you can always coat fired silver clay with a layer of gold, either in the form of slip or sheet. Gold slip is commercially available in the form of Aura 22 or Art Clay Gold Paste. It is applied in layers and can be fired over silver to add gold accents. Another way to combine silver and gold is by simply forming clay elements and firing them together. If you use Art Clay Gold, fire the gold part first, since it requires a higher sintering temperature than silver. Then add the silver clay portion to the design and fire them together, as one, at the silver clay's firing temperature. With PMC 22K Gold, you can fire silver and gold greenware pieces together, because the firing temperatures are compatible and low enough to keep the silver from melting. Of course, you can always fire the gold first and then the silver if desired, depending on what is needed for your design. All clay can always be refired and designs can be built in stages.

left: *Split Lentil Pendant* by Donna Penoyer using 22K gold. Photo by the artist.

right: *Thistle Brooch* by Nancy Hamilton with PMC, Aura 22K Gold, sterling silver pin back, and CZ stone. Photo by the artist.

Combining Gold and Silver Clays

Designs derived from nature date back to the earliest examples of gold jewelry created by artisans from ancient civilizations. Gold clay has a wonderful texture that lends itself to replicating the jewelry of ages past. Petals can be shaped, folded, and creased easily to form delicate flowers and botanical shapes. The finished pieces glow with the rich color characteristic of high-karat gold.

MATERIALS YOU'LL NEED FOR A GOLD
FLORAL PENDANT AND EARRINGS:

PMC Gold

PMC+ Silver

Basic metal clay tools (*see pages 16–18*)

$5/16$ inch (8mm) and $7/16$ inch (11mm)
    heart-shaped cutters (*Kemper Klay
    Kutters work well*)

One cubic zirconia stone

Gold jump rings

Gold chain

Gold ear wires

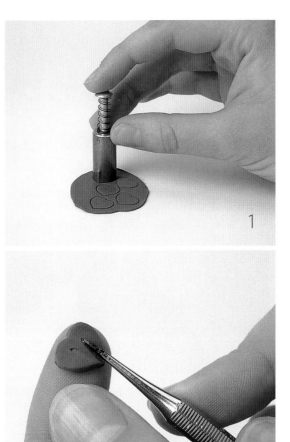

1 Roll out a thin sheet of gold metal clay about three playing cards thick. For the pendant, cut out five hearts with the $7/16$ inch (11mm) cutter. Cut out five smaller hearts with the $5/16$ inch (8mm) cutter for each earring.

2 Use a needle tool to make two grooves in a V shape on each heart to make flower petals.

3 Attach the heart petals next to each other in a cluster of five petals for the pendant and five petals for each earring. Apply water to help join the petals.

4 Use a clay shaper tool or a paintbrush to blend the points of the petals together in the center of each flower. Roll the gold metal clay into a long, skinny rope and cut off small sections, approximately ½ inch (1.3cm) long, to make a loop for each flower. Join the ends with water and a clay shaper or brush to join.

5 Attach the gold metal clay loops to the top and back of each flower with water, pressing with a clay shaper tool. Fire the flower pendant and the earrings on a flat kiln shelf (PMC 22K Gold = 1650°F [899°C] for ten minutes). After the finished pieces are cool, brush the flowers with a brass scratch brush to burnish the gold.

6 Roll a small ball of silver clay and press it into the center of each flower, using PMC+ slip to attach. Press a cubic zirconia stone into the ball of clay until the girdle of the stone is just below the surface of the clay. Texture the edges of the silver clay around the stone with a needle tool for decoration.

7 Fire the flower pieces again (PMC+ = 1650°F [899°C] for ten minutes). Finish the earrings with a brass scratch brush. Sand the edges with polishing papers until smooth.

To complete the project, attach a gold bail and hang the pendant from a gold chain and the earrings from gold ear wires.

Gold Metal Clay

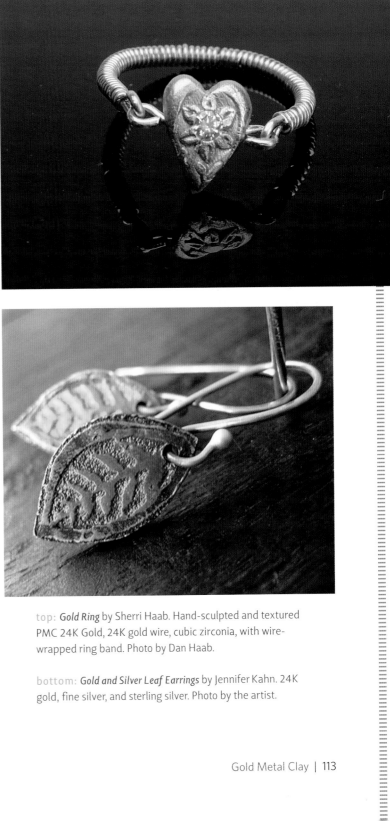

above: *Fine-Silver Pod Pendant* by Christina Leonard. Fine silver with 24K gold and patina with liver of sulfur. Photo copyright © by Jonathan David Sabin.

top: *Gold Ring* by Sherri Haab. Hand-sculpted and textured PMC 24K Gold, 24K gold wire, cubic zirconia, with wire-wrapped ring band. Photo by Dan Haab.

bottom: *Gold and Silver Leaf Earrings* by Jennifer Kahn. 24K gold, fine silver, and sterling silver. Photo by the artist.

etching

Etching is the process of removing metal, which traditionally is accomplished by using strong acids that eat away at the exposed metal. A resist is used to protect those surfaces on the metal that you do not want to etch away. Etching can be applied directly to the surface of metal clay when water- or electro-etching, or you can etch copper or brass plates that can be used as texture sheets to pattern the surface of metal clay. Etching can be applied directly to the surface of metal clay in the case of water- or electro-etching, or you can etch copper or brass plates to use as texture sheets as a tool to pattern the surface of metal clay. Etched plates provide sharper detail than textures derived from other materials such as rubber stamps.

Water-etching is the process of using water and a sponge to remove metal clay in the greenware stage (see page 20) to create a design using a resist such as wax. This method is an easy way to control the depth of the design, as you can remove as much as you want and stop etching when you are satisfied with the design. After the design is eroded away by the water, fire the piece as directed for the type of metal clay used. Adding a patina emphasizes the etched design.

Another way to etch directly onto metal clay is by electro-etching. This etching method uses an electric current and an electrolyte to remove the exposed metal. The metal that is etched away sticks, or plates, to the stainless steel pan in which the etching process takes place. Silver, bronze, and copper can all be electro-etched. Traditional methods of chemical etching will not work on metal clay due to its porosity. Because electricity is directional, it only etches in a straight line, whereas chemicals "soak" into the metal, thus disintegrating it. The best part about water- and electro-etching is that both methods are considered less harmful to the environment than chemical methods.

Water-Etching Metal Clay

Water-etching is a unique way to give dimension to metal clay. It's perfect for creating one-of-a-kind decorative surface treatments by embossing original designs onto metal clay. The water-etching method involves creating a design on clay in the greenware state with a resist such as wax. A sponge and water is used to remove the clay, which creates an etched pattern on the clay. Catherine Davies Paetz is an innovative jewelry designer who has developed her own techniques for etching on metal clay, including the swirl design featured in this earring project. These instructions are for silver clay. If you're using copper or bronze (both etch well—and wax resist works equally well for both), Catherine recommends kiln-firing to burn off the wax and binder. Although any metal clay can be water-etched, Catherine's favorite is PMC+, as it gives the sharpest lines.

MATERIALS YOU'LL NEED FOR WATER-ETCHED EARRINGS:

PMC+ Silver

Silk sponge

Two small, round watercolor paintbrushes; one for clay, and one for the wax (*sizes 0 or 1 work well*)

Water bowl, tray, or jar

Pencil

Wax resist (*Mayco brand works well; see Whole Lotta Whimsy under Resources*)

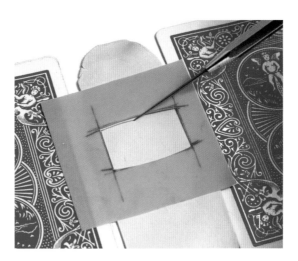

1 Make a paper template for the shape of your earrings. Roll out a sheet of clay about three or four playing cards thick. You can roll a thicker sheet of clay if a really deep etch is desired. Cut out the shapes with a knife. Pierce holes for hanging with a needle tool. Let the clay piece dry thoroughly. You can refine the holes when the clay is dry.

Safety Warning

Whenever you are burning off materials in the kiln or firing large amounts of clay, good ventilation in the studio is essential.

2 After the shapes dry, refine their edges with a nail file, sanding away scratches and imperfections.

3 Draw your design lightly with pencil. Don't worry about being precise, since the pencil lines will either wash or burn off. Don't press too hard with the pencil or you could create indentations.

4 Paint the resist onto the clay. Be sure to get complete coverage. Any gaps in coverage of your lines will be etched and appear as pits after firing. Apply wax over any areas you will be handling or want to protect while etching. (Especially cover the sides and back so you don't damage other parts of your piece by smudging the surface or accidentally removing material.) Allow the resist to dry thoroughly. Do not use a hot plate or dehydrator to accelerate drying, as this will soften the wax. When in doubt, test in a small, inconspicuous area. If you try to etch before the resist is completely dry, you risk removing some wax or disturbing your lines. Depending on the product you use, two hours is usually good, but longer or overnight is even better. Always allow more time in damp conditions.

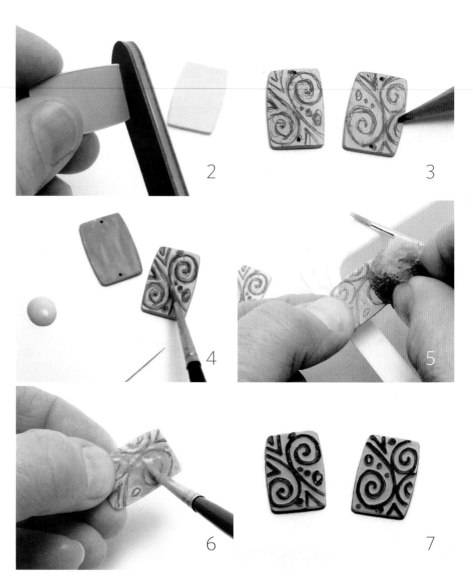

5 Fill the jar or bowl with water. Work over a clean surface like a plastic cutting board or nonstick sheet so that you can recover any clay-filled drips. Dip the sponge in the water jar and wring out most of the water, leaving a fairly wet (but not dripping) sponge. After a few passes with the sponge, you'll see how much water works best. Wipe the clay surface gently in all directions. If you only wipe in one direction, you will have a slope at the beginning of the pass and an undercut on the other. As you remove

Recycling Clay

The clay that is removed during the etching process can be reused. To do this, wait until the water becomes clear and the clay has settled. Carefully pour off the excess water. You may get some wax residue in the water, so allow the water to evaporate completely. A wax skin will form on the top of the clay. It is best to avoid this, but if it happens, peel off the wax layer before reconstituting the clay as slip or paste.

clay and it accumulates in the sponge, dip the sponge back in the jar and wring out the clay. Continue to make passes, gently removing more clay.

6 You can also use a paintbrush to loosen the clay, which works especially well if you have delicate lines. Work at a pace that doesn't allow your piece to become saturated with water, or it will become flexible and lose its form. If you notice this happening, stop and allow it to dry thoroughly before continuing. You can always do this process in stages. Keep removing clay until you are happy with the depth of the relief. Finish by leaving the surface slightly wet (but not soggy). Set the piece aside to dry until the clay no longer appears damp. By leaving the surface wet, you'll get fewer sponge marks, unless you want to add a measure of texture. If you decide you want to etch deeper after the piece dries, you can repeat the process. It's always better to stop too soon than go too far. When you are certain you have finished, the piece can then be dried on a hot plate or dehydrator.

7 When the piece is completely dry, fire at the appropriate time and temperature for the clay you are using. The wax will burn away as you fire the clay. Vent your kiln as you do this. Finish and polish as you would any other metal clay piece. Brush or tumble the pieces. Add a patina, removing the patina from the raised pattern with a polishing pad. Add earring findings and form bead dangles using head pins and pearls to complete the earrings.

Water-etched earrings by Catherine Davies Paetz. Photo by Sherri Haab.

Electro-Etching Metal Clay

Etching metal is a well-known jewelry-making technique. The most common method of etching involves a chemical called ferric chloride. This chemical doesn't work very well for etching copper or bronze metal clay, because metal clay is porous and the ferric chloride chews through the metal and erodes it in every direction. With electro-etching you can etch silver, copper, and bronze clays in a controlled fashion due to the fact that electricity travels in a straight line, giving you predicable results. This project uses an electrolyte combined with electricity, which avoids the need for hazardous disposal issues or harmful chemical fumes. Copper sulfate is used for copper and bronze clays; for silver clay, use 10 grams of silver nitrate instead. Be sure to review the safety precautions below before handling copper sulfate.

MATERIALS YOU'LL NEED FOR AN
ELECTRO-ETCHED COPPER CLAY HEART:

Copper metal clay

Basic metal clay tools (see pages 16–18)

Round glass form to dry clay on (a light
    bulb works well)

E3 Etch electronic controller kit™ (see
Resources, under www.sherrihaab.com)

Stainless steel pan (comes with E3
    Etch kit)

Two 18-gauge aluminum wire electrodes
    (comes with E3 Etch kit)

Copper sulfate (comes with E3 Etch kit)

Four foam spacers (comes with E3 Etch kit)
    to suspend the copper in the pan

Packing tape

600-grit sandpaper

Rubbing alcohol

Cotton swabs

Water (use distilled water if you have hard
    water)

Oil-based paint marker (Sharpie works
    well), or fingernail polish

Embossing heat tool

Acetone

1 Roll out a thick sheet of copper metal
  clay. Cut out a large heart shape with

Handling Copper Sulfate

Copper sulfate is commonly used to maintain pipes and keep tap roots from growing into them. Keep copper sulfate away from children and pets, as it is hazardous to ingest. Because it can also be an irritant to skin and eyes, avoid contact by wearing rubber gloves and eye protection. Copper sulfate can be reused and stored in liquid form, but strain it through a coffee filter to remove any debris. If you choose not to reuse it, the amount used in the kit can be disposed of by flushing it away.

a craft knife. Use a needle tool to pierce a hole on each side for hanging. Place the heart over a curved surface, such as a light bulb or glass ball, to dry. Let the piece dry for at least a day. Remove from the curved surface and continue to air dry until dry on both sides. Refine the holes with a knife and smooth the edges by sanding. Fire the piece according to copper clay firing directions on page 39.

2 After the piece is fired and cooled, burnish with a brass scratch brush. Prepare the surface prior to etching by sanding it with 600-grit sandpaper. This will give the metal some tooth to help the resist adhere. After sanding, clean the surface with rubbing alcohol using a cotton swab. Dry the piece, and avoid touching the surface. Use a paint marker to create a design on the metal. You can use a pencil to mark the design prior to using the marker.

3 To prepare your copper for etching, paint around the edges of the piece with the marker. Set the paint by heating it with an embossing heat tool. This will help the paint to adhere during the etching process. Alternatively you can "draw" or mask off with nail polish instead of the marker. After the paint dries, apply a piece of tape covering just part of the piece on the backside as shown. Part of the copper is left exposed in this step to allow you to add the electrode wire described in the next step.

4 Bend one of the aluminum wires enclosed in the E3 Etch kit into a soft 90-degree angle or L shape at about the middle of the wire. Make sure the bend is not too sharp, as it may cause corrosion at the bend. Do not use pliers to make the bend; use your fingers to ensure a rounded bend. This wire will serve as an electrode to conduct the electricity. Make a few short bends at the end of the wire in a zigzag or S shape as shown. Position the zigzag end onto the exposed part of the copper. The metals must touch to properly conduct, so make sure you are placing the wire below the tape on bare copper. Place a second piece of tape over the wire to hold it in place and to ensure good contact. The tape will also protect the copper from the etching solution. Fold the edges of the tape over or trim close to the edge. At this stage, the entire back and sides of the copper should be taped or masked off.

Electro-etching is ideal for metal clay, as it does not erode the metal as chemical etchants do. Copper clay heart by Sherri Haab.

5 Mix the etching solution. (Caution: Keep the supplies away from children and pets, as it is hazardous to ingest.) Mix and dissolve 4 teaspoons (24g) of the granular powder into 12 ounces (350ml) of warm water in a stainless steel pan. Do this in advance to give the crystals time to dissolve. It is not critical that the amounts are precise; you may use more or less water. (Note: Use distilled water if you have hard water. Hard water interferes with the etching process.) Attach the foam spacers around the shape being etched to suspend it so it's level with the bottom of the pan. Make sure the foam does not cover any part of the copper you wish to etch. Note how tape was used to attach the foam spacers to avoid disturbing the design.

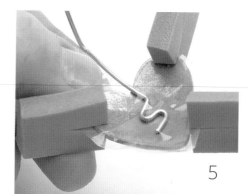

6 Attach the black controller clip to the pan and the red clip to the end of the electrode. Set the copper piece in the bottom of the pan, spacers touching the bottom, and the design face down. The spacers will suspend and keep the copper from touching the bottom of the pan during etching. The spacers are not supposed to float. If the piece is small and starts to float, weight it down by draping a towel, booklet, or similar object over the pan to hold the piece close to the bottom. The copper needs to be about ½ inch (1.3cm) from the bottom of the pan with the spacers sitting on the bottom of the pan for proper conductivity. Set the E3 Etch controller on "Fast Etch." Turn the power on. (The green light will indicate that the power is on.) The red light will indicate that the clips are properly attached. If the red light does not appear, check to make sure that plastic or tape is not interfering with the copper and wire contacts. Wait for two to four hours for the etching to occur. Resist the urge to check the progress too frequently, as moving the piece repeatedly may disturb the resist. Carefully tip the piece out to check after a few hours and ease it back into the solution to continue etching if more depth is desired. Turn the power off and unclip the wire when complete.

7 After etching, rinse the piece off and dry it. Remove the toner with acetone using a cotton swab.

8 Finish the metal as desired. This piece was simply burnished with a stainless steel scratch brush and burnishing tool to bring out the shine on the high spots.

9 Add a patina to darken the recessed areas. Use a polishing pad to remove the patina from the raised areas.

Electro-Etching Texture Plates

Make your own texture plates by electro-etching original designs onto copper, which then can be used to texture any type of metal clay. Choose a graphic design or pattern that's been photocopied or printed out with black toner and then apply it to a sheet of copper. The metal will be etched wherever it is exposed. You can find designs in clip art books, or create your own original design. I copied and reduced my name to etch on a metal plate to create a signature stamp. I use this etched design to impress my signature into the metal clay to make small metal hangtags to attach to my finished pieces (see page 125 for an example). In addition to the methods described here using toner, you can mask the metal with tape or stickers or use an oil-based paint pen (see Electro-Etching Metal Clay on page 118). The finished metal plates will quickly become one of your favorite tools for adding texture to metal clay. Be sure to review the safety precautions on page 118 before handling copper sulfate.

MATERIALS YOU'LL NEED FOR TEXTURE PLATES:

E3 Etch electronic controller kit *(see Resources, under www.sherrihaab.com)*

Stainless steel pan *(comes with E3 Etch kit)*

Two 18-gauge aluminum wire electrodes *(comes with E3 Etch kit)*

Copper sulfate *(comes with E3 Etch kit)*

Four foam spacers *(comes with E3 Etch kit)* to suspend the copper in the pan

One 2½ by 2½ inch (6 by 6cm) 22-gauge copper square *(comes with E3 Etch kit)*

Black laser-toner image printed on E3 Etch paper

Oil-based paint marker *(Sharpie works well)*, or fingernail polish

Household iron

Wooden board for ironing

Press cloth *(an old pillowcase works well)*

Embossing heat tool

Packing tape

600-grit sandpaper

Rubbing alcohol

Cotton swabs

Water *(use distilled water if you have hard water)*

Acetone

Etched copper texture plates, including hand-scripted designs for metal clay. Plates by Sherri Haab

1   If your copper plate has a protective coating, peel it off
    before sanding! Prepare the copper blank by sanding it with
600-grit paper. This will give the metal some "tooth" to help the
resist to adhere. After sanding, clean the surface with rubbing
alcohol using a cotton swab. Dry the piece, and avoid touching
the surface.

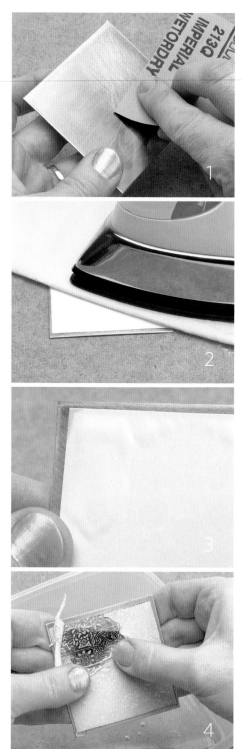

2   For a direct toner transfer method, print a black-and-white
    design onto E3 Etch laser paper using a toner-based laser
copier. Choose a design with strong lines and crisp details.
The black areas of the design will act as a resist in the etching
solution. Cut the design to fit your copper blank. Hint: Since
the copper plate will be used as a tool to transfer textures or
designs to metal clay, print the image (such as text) correctly
oriented. The image will etch in reverse on the copper, which will
allow it to be correctly oriented in the finished clay texture. To
transfer the image to the copper, place the copper on a wooden
board and place the image face down on the copper. Use a press
cloth, or old pillowcase, to cover the paper, being careful not to
displace. Press the piece with an iron, on a high setting (cotton
or linen). Press with firm pressure for about one to two minutes,
covering the entire piece to ensure even heating.

3   Check the piece to make sure the paper is adhered
    properly. The paper should be flat with no ripples where
the toner was heated and fused. You may see ripples or bubbles
where the toner is not present. You can press longer to make
sure it is properly heated for the transfer. Designs with more
toner tend to be easier to work with than designs with very little.
Designs with fine lines are more difficult to transfer. You can
always print the design as the inverse, thus providing more toner
to the design and less copper to etch.

4   After ironing the image onto the metal, let the metal
    cool well. Soak the piece in water until the paper looks
transparent without white spots. This takes about ten minutes
but can sit longer. Carefully roll the paper, working from the
center out with your fingers. Redip the piece in water to moisten
if needed. Don't scrape or scratch, or you may remove the toner.
Simply rub the paper off until you can see the design. Don't
worry if a white haze is left behind on the design; it is just paper
fibers left behind which won't affect the etching. Better to leave
the fibers than to risk scratching off part of the design. Pat the
piece dry with a cloth or towel.

5 If you accidentally lose some of the image, you can use a paint marker to fill in the missing parts. If sections of the design did not transfer, use a marker to color in the areas. Nail polish also works very well as a resist. If your transfer didn't work, you can always sand the piece and start again. Heat the pen and toner with an embossing heat tool, which will keep the ink from flaking off during etching.

6 To prepare the piece for etching, you must add an electrode and tape the metal where you don't want to etch. Cover half of the back of the copper with a piece of tape. Add an aluminum wire to conduct the electricity, placing it over the part of the copper that is still exposed on the back. Bend one of the aluminum wires enclosed in the kit into a soft 90-degree angle or L shape at about the middle of the wire to make a stem extending from the back. Make sure the bend is not too sharp, as it may cause corrosion at the bend. Do not use pliers to make the bend; use your fingers to ensure a rounded bend. The wire will serve as an electrode to conduct the electricity. Make a few short bends at the end of the wire in a zigzag or S shape as shown. Position the zigzag end onto the exposed part of the copper. The metals must touch to properly conduct, so make sure you are placing the wire on bare copper and not over the tape.

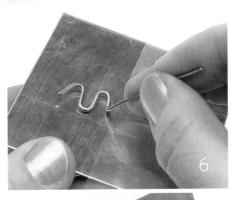

7 Place tape over the wire to secure it and also to cover the remainder of the metal on the back of the piece.

8 Trim the tape about ½ inch (1.3cm) from the edge of the metal. Fold the tape over the edge a bit to protect the edges from etching.

9 Mix the etching solution. (Caution: Keep the supplies away from children and pets, as it is hazardous to ingest.) Mix and dissolve 4 teaspoons (24g) of the granular powder into 12 ounces (350ml) of water in a stainless steel pan. Do this in advance to give the crystals time to dissolve. It is not critical that the amounts are precise; you may use more or less water. (Note: Use distilled water if you have hard water. Hard water interferes with the etching process.) Attach the foam spacers around the shape being etched, to suspend it so it is level with the bottom of the pan. Make sure the foam does not cover any part of the copper you wish to etch. If you would like to keep the spacers away from the copper, simply make tabs with folded tape and attach the spacers to the tape tabs.

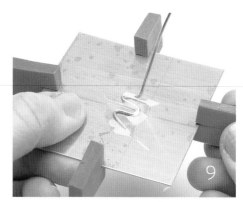

10 Attach the black controller clip to the pan and the red clip to the end of the electrode. Set the copper piece in the bottom of the pan with the spacers touching the bottom and the design face down. The spacers will suspend and keep the copper from touching the bottom of the pan during etching. The copper needs to be about ½ inch (1.3cm) from the bottom of the pan with the spacers sitting on the bottom of the pan for proper conductivity. Set the E3 Etch controller on "Fast Etch." Turn the power on (the green light will indicate it is on). The red light will indicate that the clips are properly attached. If the red light does not appear, check to make sure that plastic or tape is not interfering with the copper and wire contacts. Wait for two to four hours for the etching to occur. Resist the urge to check the progress too frequently, as moving the piece repeatedly may disturb the resist. Carefully tip the piece out to check after a few hours and ease it back into the solution to continue etching if more depth is desired. Turn the power off and unclip the wire when complete.

11 After etching, rinse the piece off and dry it. Remove the toner with acetone nail polish and a cotton swab.

12 Use the finished texture plates to texture metal clay. Oil the plate slightly if needed to keep the clay from sticking to the etched metal.

Etched Metal Clay

above: *Bronze Pendant* by Sherri Haab. Etched design on copper, brass chain, glass bead, and copper wire. Photo by the artist.

top: *Pillow Bead* by Emma Baird. Fine-silver textured with etched copper plate, pearls, and sterling silver clasp. Photo by the artist.

below: *Signature Hang Tag for Jewelry* by Sherri Haab. Name embossed (see page 121) on silver using etched copper plate. Fine silver, resin, paper, ribbon, and sterling silver. Photo by Dan Haab.

epoxy resin

Epoxy resin is often referred to as "cold enameling," and is an alternative to using traditional glass enamels on metal. Epoxy resin is easy to use, inexpensive, and readily available in craft or hardware stores. Envirotex Lite®, Colores™, and Devcon 2-Ton® Clear Epoxy are a few brand names. Some brands are clear and some add color to the resin. There is a wide range of techniques you can experiment with to achieve interesting effects with the resin. By adding fillers and dyes, you can simulate glass and certain stones such as amber and granite, just to name a few.

Various powders, liquid dyes, and pigments can be added to clear resin to add texture and color. Add a little to create a translucent color, or a bit more for an opaque mixture. Other materials can be layered or mixed in, such as glitter, sand, gold or silver leaf, paper images, or rhinestones. Liquids such as oil paints may react with the resin, so it is best to stick with dry materials or liquid dyes and pigments made especially for resin.

Epoxy resin is sold in a two-part mixture. Resin and a hardener (catalyst) are mixed together thoroughly and then applied to the form. The resin will cure at room temperature, curing faster in a warm area. The proportions for mixing vary from brand to brand. Follow the manufacturer's instructions carefully for success. Experiment with the formulas that mix with a 1:1 ratio, which are the easiest to use. After mixing the batch of resin, colorants can be added, or it can be left clear to be layered over images for a glasslike effect.

Using Clear Epoxy Resin

Tiny pictures set in handmade silver frames are a great way to preserve memories. Clear resin protects the images and looks like glass in the frames. Reduce photos to fit the frames by scanning them and then resizing with a photo program. The finished framed images make great charms for bracelets and necklaces for Mother's Day, birthdays, baby showers, or wedding gifts.

MATERIALS YOU'LL NEED FOR A PICTURE FRAME:

Silver metal clay

Basic metal clay tools (*see pages 16–18*)

Small cutters (*smaller cutter for the inside of the frame and a larger one for the outside*)

Small, reduced images

Mod Podge® decoupage glue

Paintbrush

Patina (*optional*)

Two-part epoxy resin (*Envirotex Lite works well*)

Toothpicks or old paintbrush

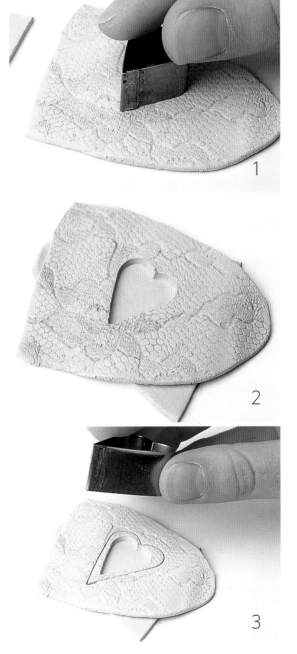

1 Roll out a thin sheet of clay about two to three playing cards thick. Cut the sheet in half to make a sheet for the base and one for the frame. Texture the frame sheet. Cut out the inside shape of the frame from the textured clay with a small clay cutter.

2 Brush water between the two sheets of clay and place the cut textured sheet on top of the base sheet. Press the layers to adhere.

3 Use the larger cutter to cut out the frame through both layers of clay. Use oil to prevent the cutter from sticking. Check to make sure the cut is even all the way around the frame. Remove any excess clay.

4   Use a needle tool to make a hole in the top of the frame. If you do not have room to make a hole, you can insert a fine-silver eyelet or make a clay loop instead. Let the frame dry on a flat surface until bone-dry. Sand the edges of the frame with a nail file until smooth. Fire the frame on a kiln shelf according to the type of clay you are using (see pages 36–37). Finish the frame with a brass scratch brush and burnishing tool to bring out the shine on raised areas. Apply a patina to the frame if desired before gluing the image in place.

5   Reduce the image on a copier or printer. Seal both sides of the image with a coating of glue using a paintbrush. Let the glue dry.

6   Cut the image to fit inside the frame. Hint: If you press a scrap piece of paper into the finished frame, you can see where the paper conforms to the edges of the frame. The paper can then be cut to use as a pattern. Apply glue around the cut edge of the image and then press it into the frame.

7 Mix the two-part epoxy resin according to the manufacturer's instructions. Use a toothpick or an old paintbrush to add a layer of resin to coat the surface. Let the piece cure (preferably in a warm room to speed curing). Refer to the manufacturer's instructions for more details on curing the epoxy resin.

8 Add a jump ring after the resin has cured. To make a necklace, hang the frame from a chain. You can also attach multiple frames to make a charm bracelet.

To make a necklace, hang the frames from a chain. You can also attach multiple frames to make charm bracelets.

Coloring Epoxy Resin

Epoxy resin enamel can be used to simulate glass enamel. Pigment powders are added to the resin for color and opacity. Epoxy can be mixed just like paint to create any hue. Choose three primary colors to start with, mixing a range of colors for a pleasing palette. If you make a mistake, simply remove the resin from the surface with a cotton swab or paper towel before the resin cures, and reapply.

MATERIALS YOU'LL NEED FOR AN
EPOXY RESIN ENAMEL TIE CLIP:

Silver clay

Basic metal clay tools (*see pages 16–18*)

Rubber stamp block (*see Resources under
Speedy Stamp™ Blocks, Speedball® Art
    Products*)

V-shaped medium line cutter (*Speedball
    #2 works well*)

Two-part epoxy resin (*Envirotex Lite
    works well*)

Pigment powders (*Pearl Ex Powders
    work well*)

Toothpicks

Quick-setting two-part epoxy resin
    (*Devcon 2-Ton Epoxy resin works well*)

Tie clip

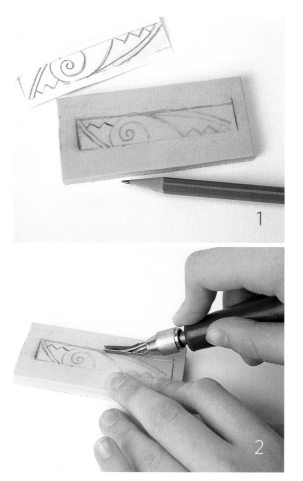

1 Draw a geometric design with paper and pencil that is ½ inch (1.3cm) wide by 2¾ inches (7cm) long. Rub the image face down onto the rubber stamp block to transfer.

2 Use a V-shaped cutting tool to carve the lines of the design following the manufacturer's instructions for carving. The carving will serve as the mold for the reversed raised edges needed on the silver clay. The raised areas will surround and form the cavities for the two-part epoxy resin.

3 Roll out a sheet of clay about five playing cards thick. Lightly oil the clay and the carved mold to prevent sticking. Press the sheet of clay onto the mold and roll again to make sure the clay is in full contact with the surface of the mold.

4 Lift the clay from the carved mold and trim around the edges, making any repairs necessary. Let the clay dry. Sand the edges lightly with a nail file to smooth the edges. Place the piece flat on a kiln shelf and fire according to the type of silver clay used (see pages 36–37). Finish the silver metal piece with a brass scratch brush and sanding papers. For a brighter finish, continue polishing with progressive polishing papers or tumble for a mirror finish.

5 Mix several colors of epoxy resin enamel. Start by mixing equal parts of a hardener and the resin. Add pigment powders to color the resin. Make sure mixtures are carefully measured and stirred according to the manufacturer's instructions. Be sure to wear a dust mask for safety while working with the powders.

6 Fill the cavities of the finished silver with the colored resin using a toothpick. Let the piece cure in a warm place for at least twenty-four hours or until hard to the touch. If it is tacky, let the piece continue to cure. The finished piece can be left as is or sanded for a matte finish. Sand in water using progressive grits of wet/dry sandpapers. Start with 220-grit, working up to 600-grit or higher. Finish with buffing and polishing to bring a shine back to the resin and silver. Use quick-setting epoxy resin to glue a tie clip to the back.

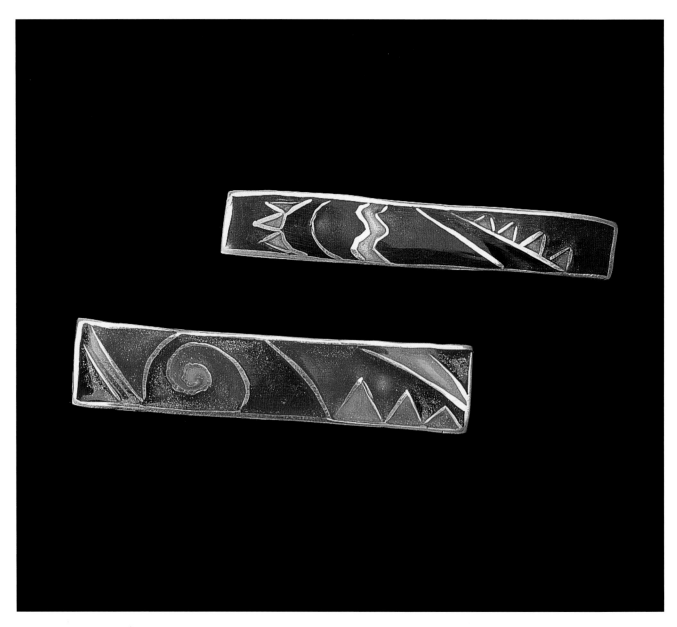

Fine silver and epoxy resin tie clips by Sherri Haab. Photo by Dan Haab.

Epoxy Resin with Metal Clay

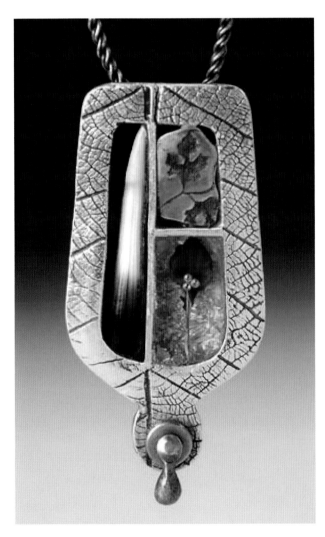

above: *Woodland Altar* by Lora Hart. Box construction techniques with UV resin. Porcupine quill, bronze clay shard, pinecone, and miniglass balls. Photo by Marsha Thomas.

top right: *Virgen de Guadalupe Nicho* by Lorena Angulo. PMC3 fabricated nicho image taken from an original painting by the artist, and printed on photo paper and covered with resin. Nicho decorated with red coral beads, hand-sculpted PMC3 heart milagro, and a sterling silver chain. Photo by George Post.

bottom: *Silver Pins* by Catherine Witherell. Clear resin, 22K gold balls, fine-silver clay, hand-constructed PMC+, resin, Swarovski crystal rhinestones and fireball, 22K gold, fine silver, soldered sterling silver findings on back. Photo by the artist.

color
on metal

There are a number of ways to add color to a finished metal clay piece. Glass enameling is a well-known technique for adding color to fine silver, gold, and copper finished clays. In addition to glass enamels, there are modern materials such as resin, acrylic mediums, polymer clay, colored pencils, and dyes that add color to the finished metal clay. Many of these materials are simply applied to the surface of the fired and finished metal clay with minimal effort. The combination of surface preparation techniques and heat curing will help with the permanency of the medium you choose.

Using polymer clay is a great way to incorporate color into your metal clay work. Polymer clay must be conditioned after opening. To condition polymer clay, knead it with your hands until it is soft. A favorite tool of polymer clay artists is a pasta roller, which is used to roll nice, even sheets of clay. This tool should be dedicated only for use with polymer clay, and should not come into contact with any food-handling items.

Bake polymer clay on a glass baking dish or a ceramic tile in an oven. For those who use polymer clay frequently, it's best to use a toaster oven solely dedicated to it. Most brands can be baked at 275°F (135°C) for thirty minutes. Let the clay cool in the oven for a stronger finished product. Polymer clay emits toxic fumes if fired above the temperature given by the manufacturer's instructions.

Uncured polymer clay can be baked directly onto the finished metal clay piece. The polymer clay will be very hot after baking, as it conducts heat well. After the pieces are finished, you can finish the polymer and metal clays together with sanding and buffing. Because polymer clay is softer than metal clay, it's helpful to complete most of the metal clay finishing before adding the polymer clay. Save the final polishing until after the polymer clay has been cured.

Acrylic mediums, glass paints, and dyes are applied to the finished metal clay with a paintbrush. Thin the mediums for watercolor effects with less opacity. Because metal clay is porous in its unburnished state, the paint adheres to the surface. Heating between 275°F (135°C) to 325°F (163°C) sets most acrylic paints and mediums.

Colored pencils and waxes are also used by artists to add color to metals. Wax is thinned with solvents that "melt" the wax for painterly effects on metal. Layering colored pencil on metal gives depth and rich color to the surface.

Faux Cloisonné with Polymer Clay

Choose simple graphic designs to make metal clay cloisonné. Look in clip-art or graphic design books and rubber stamp catalogs for inspiration. Designs can be simplified and changed by hand or on a photocopier. Experiment with colored pencils on copies until you are pleased with your design and color selections before making this project.

MATERIALS YOU'LL NEED FOR A
CLOISONNÉ PIN:

Art Clay Silver

Basic metal clay tools (see pages 16–18)

Rubber stamp block (Speedy Stamp
    Blocks, Speedball Art Products,
    see Resources)

V-shaped medium cutter (Speedball
    #2 works well)

Red, yellow, and blue polymer clay
    (Premo™ works well)

Polymer clay tools, including pasta roller
    (to make thin sheets of clay)

Sobo, or other PVA white glue

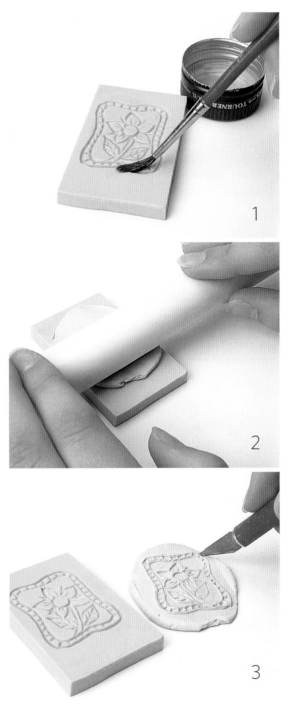

1 Transfer a pencil drawing by rubbing the design face down on a rubber stamp block. Carve the design deeply with a V-shaped cutter into the rubber block. Use a paintbrush to coat the carved rubber block with oil. Make sure to oil all of the grooves in the carving to keep the clay from sticking.

2 Roll out a thick sheet of metal clay. Press the sheet of clay onto the mold and roll again to make sure the clay is in full contact with the surface of the mold.

3 Peel the metal clay away from the carving. Use an X-Acto blade to trim around the edges. Add loops of clay onto the bottom of the pin with slip, if you desire. Dry the pin on a flat surface

Silver and polymer clay pin by Sherri Haab. Photo by Dan Haab.

Applying Pigments to Metal Clay

There are many ways to add color to a finished metal clay piece. Artists use glass enamels, polymer clay, colored pencils, and paint, just to name a few. I have found that ITS™ image transfer medium works exceptionally well as a base for making your own glass and metal paints. By mixing pigment powders with the medium, you can create a range of transparent and opaque colors that mimic glass enamels. This is one way to apply bright colors such as bright pink, orange, yellows, and reds to silver colors not easily obtained unless using lead-based glass enamels. I prefer to use Pearl Ex pigment powders to make the paints, as they contain mica, which adds an iridescent quality that looks more like enamel than plain pigments. If you heat-set the dried paints on the finished metal clay, the paint takes on a glasslike quality, and the final product is durable and hard to scratch off.

MATERIALS YOU'LL NEED FOR LACE BEADS:
PMC3
Basic metal clay tools *(see pages 16–18)*
Lace for texture
Cork clay *(see page 63)*
Sobo, or PVA white glue
ITS image and color transfer solution
Pearl Ex pigment powders
Rubber stamp embossing tool
Toothpicks
Wax paper
Small disposable round paintbrush

1 Make bead cores with cork clay. Roll round balls of the cork clay with your hands and let the balls dry well, even for several days to ensure they are dry. Coat the outside of each bead core with a thin layer of glue. This will help the metal clay stick to the cork clay and also seals the cork clay from absorbing moisture from the metal clay. After the bead cores are dry, prepare the metal clay to cover the bead cores. Roll out a sheet of clay about three to four playing cards thick. Press and roll lace over the sheet to emboss texture into the metal clay. Use a cutter to cut a star or flower shape.

2 Wrap the cut shape around a single bead core (it helps to complete one at a time to keep the metal clay from drying too quickly).

3 Shape the metal clay, leaving an opening in the form.

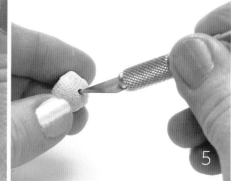

4 Pierce a hole in the center of the metal clay bead, stopping when you hit the cork clay bead core. This will serve as a pilot hole, which will be refined later, so don't worry if it is too large for stringing at this point.

5 Complete the rest of the metal clay beads. Let them dry on a hot plate or air dry. Refine the holes in the beads with the tip of a knife. Rotate the knife around like a drill to shave out the holes.

6 Use a nail file or sanding paper to refine the bead edges as needed.

7 Set the beads on a flat kiln shelf. Cradle them in fiber blanket if the beads are large. Fire them at 1470°F (799°C) for thirty minutes in an enclosed kiln. After firing and cooling, burnish the outside of the beads with a brass scratch brush and burnishing tool to brighten the texture of the lace. (I left the inside of the beads white and unburnished.)

8 To add color to the beads, mix a small amount of pigment powder with ITS image solution using a mixing stick, or toothpick, on a piece of wax paper.

9 Paint the inside of the beads with the metal paint using a small round paintbrush.

10 Rinse the paintbrush out and mix other colors for the outside of the beads. As the paint begins to dry (ten to thirty minutes after application), you can scrape some of it off to reveal the metal clay underneath as desired. Burnishing with a stainless steel tool will also bring out some of the metal clay after the paint dries.

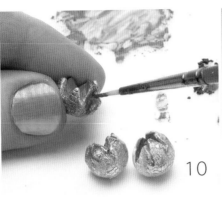

11 To set the paints, heat them with a rubber stamp embossing tool. Heat for about one to two minutes. This will cause the paints to become more transparent, like glass enamel. Let the beads cool.

These beads by Sherri Haab were made using ITS mixed with pigment powders to create custom metal paints for silver beads.

Color on Metal

above: *Tribal Sun Pendant* by Liz Hall. Fine silver and polymer clay. Photo by the artist.

top: *Pin* by Debra Weld. Layered colored pencil on PMC Silver clay. Photo by the artist.

bottom: *Bracelet* by Wendy Wallin Malinow. Silver metal clay, sterling silver, polymer clay, colored resin, pearls, and glass beads. Photo by Sherri Haab.

glass

Certain types of glass can be incorporated with unfired silver metal clay, or applied to finished silver as you would for enameling. Silver metal clay is ideal for enameling, because it is fine silver. Fine silver has a beautiful pure color that shines through transparent glass enamels. PMC3 and Art Clay Silver 650 work especially well because they fire at lower temperatures than the other types of metal clay. Their temperatures are compatible with the temperatures needed to heat and anneal the glass without melting it into a pool in the kiln.

You can texture metal clay with rubber stamps or other objects before it is fired to create cells to fill with enamel, which is easier than traditional methods of soldering wires to form cells. The finished piece simulates cloisonné and basse-taille enameling. Using metal clay opens the door for new methods and surface treatments to which enamels can be applied. The enameling project on page 152 features Champlevé enameling, which is a great project for beginners.

Some considerations need to be taken into account when working with glass. All glass is sensitive to heat. If glass is heated or cooled too quickly, it will crack. The kiln must be ramped up at a rate that allows the glass to adjust to the heat. After firing the piece, the glass must be cooled slowly to prevent thermal shock from cracking the glass. This can be accomplished by leaving the kiln door shut until the glass piece has cooled completely. Glass must be annealed when it is heated or fired. Annealing stabilizes the glass to prevent strain on it and is accomplished through proper heating and cooling. Annealing temperatures and length of time is determined by the type of glass used, and by the thickness of the glass. Larger pieces need to be annealed for longer periods of time. Refer to annealing charts provided by glass manufacturers.

If glass is held at high temperatures and for long enough, it can cause devitrification. This causes the surface of the glass to become cloudy and rough as the glass changes to a crystalline condition. Most types of glass used for kiln work are formulated to minimize the chance of devitrification.

By using the proper glass combined with PMC3 or Art Clay Silver 650 for a project, there is little chance of failure. As long as you use low firing temperatures and monitor the heating and cooling of the glass, you should be successful. Dichroic glass cabochons are a great way to combine glass with metal clay. The dichroic glass bookmark project on page 144 is made with a small to medium size dichroic glass cabochon. Dichroic glass has a surface layer consisting of fine metal particles. To make cabochons, layers of dichroic glass are fused together and annealed to make "gemlike" shapes out of the glass. Dichroic glass cabochons made with Bullseye or Uroboros® glass can easily be fired with silver metal clay. Metal clay can be used to surround a cabochon to make bezels that frame the glass, and both can be fired together to make jewelry or functional items emphasizing the beauty of the glass.

Firing Glass with Metal Clay

A dichroic cabochon sparkles like a gem when set in a silver bezel. Glass artists who specialize in making dichroic glass cabochons combine color and pattern to create beautiful combinations. Choosing a glass cabochon can give you inspiration for designing a metal clay project. This bookmark is a way to make something other than jewelry and is a great way to feature glass in your work.

MATERIALS YOU'LL NEED FOR A DICHROIC GLASS BOOKMARK:

PMC3 silver metal clay

Basic metal clay tools (*see pages 16–18*)

Texturing object or tool

¾ to 1-inch (2–2.5cm) dichroic glass cabochon

Rubbing alcohol and swab

Bullseye ThinFire Paper

2-inch (5cm) piece of 20-gauge sterling or fine silver wire

⅝-inch (1.6cm) wide ribbon 12 inches (30cm) long

1 Roll out a sheet of clay the thickness of a mat board or five playing cards thick. Texture the clay with a texturing object or tool (a shell was used in this project).

2 Place the dichroic cabochon in the center of the sheet of clay and cut around it using a sharp knife.

3 Remove the cutout piece of clay in the center to make a bezel to frame the cabochon. Replace the cabochon. Don't worry about a tight fit; the clay will shrink around the glass. Just make sure the cabochon fits with a little breathing room.

4　Trim the clay to make a border at least ¼ inch (6mm) to frame the cabochon. It can be cut in any shape. Use the design of the cabochon for inspiration.

5　Roll a skinny clay snake and moisten it with water. Place it around the cabochon for a loose fit. Drape the clay snake around the cabochon to fit without stretching or pulling the clay. Cut the ends bluntly and seal with water to join. Smooth the seam well for a strong bezel.

6　Bend the sterling silver wire to fit the width of the ribbon.

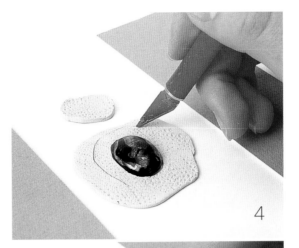

4

5

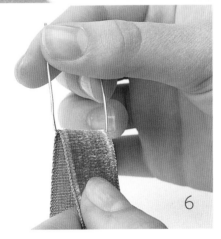

6

7 Bend the wire on each side to anchor the embedded wire in the clay. Clip off any excess wire on each side.

8 Push the wire well into the clay, leaving enough room to loop the ribbon through after firing.

9 Embellish the bezel with small pieces of clay, attaching with water and using texturing tools to decorate. Let the piece dry completely. Use a nail file to smooth the edges.

10 Clean the glass cabochon surface with a cotton swab dipped in rubbing alcohol. Make sure you remove clay dust and fingerprints. Follow the firing directions below. After firing, brush the finished piece with a brass scratch brush. Attach a ribbon by looping the end through the sterling silver wire. Sew or glue the ribbon to hold. Cut the end of the ribbon at an angle to prevent fraying.

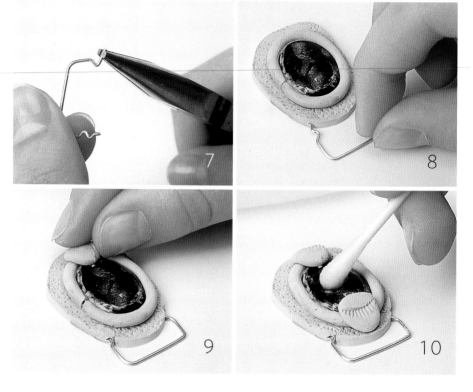

Firing the Dichroic Glass Bookmark

Hold the piece by the edges to keep the glass clean, and place the bookmark on a piece of Bullseye ThinFire paper on a flat kiln shelf. The paper will keep the back of the glass cabochon smooth as it fires. **Caution:** Do not fire glass with a torch, as it could shatter, sending glass pieces flying. Use a kiln, following all safety precautions and wearing eye protection when opening the kiln.

Set the ramp speed of the kiln to 1500°F (816°C) per hour. This temperature is slow enough to heat the glass uniformly to prevent cracking. The ramp speed is based on a cabochon that is about 1/3 inch (8mm) thick. Fire the piece at 1290°F (699°C) for ten minutes. For small- and medium-size cabochons, you can turn off the kiln at this point and let the piece cool slowly, leaving the door shut completely until cooled. The firing and the retained heat in the kiln during cooling should be sufficient to anneal a small dichroic cabochon.

For large cabochons, a longer annealing time may be required. Refer to tables and charts from the glass manufacturer for annealing information. Let the piece continue to cool. Open the door to remove the piece after it has cooled completely.

Dichroic glass cabochon by Sherry Fotopoulos. Photo by Dan Haab.

Creating Bead Caps for Lampworked Beads

This project by Lisa Blackwell uses metal clay to customize bead caps to fit lampwork glass beads. Lisa is a talented jewelry artist who combines metal, glass, resin, and other materials to create mixed-media jewelry designs. She adds textures to metal clay to make unique bead caps using silver metal clay to accent the beads. You could also use bronze or copper clay to make bead caps using this technique.

MATERIALS YOU'LL NEED FOR
A LAMPWORKED BEAD CAP:
PMC3 Silver clay
Basic metal clay tools *(see pages 16–18)*
Rubber stamps for texture
Large- and medium-size round cutters
    (size 2 round Kemper Klay Kutter
    works well)
Drinking straw
Sterling silver tubing
Riveting tool
Chasing hammer
Jeweler's saw with blade
Steel bench block
Glass beads

1 Roll out a sheet of clay about three playing cards thick. Texture the surface with a rubber stamp or other texturing tool. Use oil on the surface of the rubber stamp to prevent it from sticking to the metal clay. Cut out two large circles and two medium-size circles using the round cutters. Cut out two small circles using the drinking straw.

2 Layer the smaller round pieces onto the larger ones using a little water to adhere the layers. Press the clay layers well to ensure the layers stick together.

3 With the straw, make a hole in the center of each cap.

4 Remove the clay from the straw by pushing it out with the tip of a needle tool.

5 Divide the clay removed from each center into three tiny pieces. Using one finger to roll the clay, roll each piece into a ball in the palm of your hand. Set the six balls aside, as they will be used later to decorate the bead caps.

6 Place the clay caps onto your bead at each end with a hole.

7 Place the clay cap over the bead's hole, pressing gently to form the clay over the curved surface of the bead.

8 With a small brush, refine the edges and seams of the clay caps.

9 Use a needle tool to make three random indentations into the caps.

10 Attach the small clay balls to the caps with slip, pressing the balls into the depressions. Use a paintbrush to clean up any extra slip around the edges.

11 Place the capped bead on a hot plate to dry. When dry, the caps will fall off the bead, or you can wiggle them off. Once the caps are off the bead, let them continue to dry for at least another ten minutes.

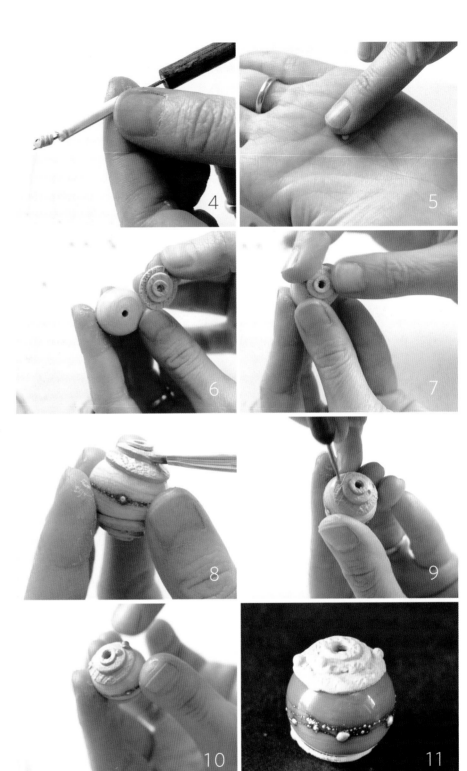

12 After the bead caps dry, you can carve the edges. Refine the edges with a file. Fire the caps. Finish by tumbling or burnishing. Apply a patina to the finished silver if desired. Polish off the raised surface, leaving the patina in the recessed textures.

13 Use sterling silver tubing in a diameter that fits through the hole of the caps and bead. Slide the tubing through the cap, bead, and second cap to determine the length you will need to cut the tubing. A very small amount of tubing should be left on either side. If the tubing is too long, it won't fit tightly to the bead.

14 Mark the sterling silver tubing with your jewelry saw and remove the bead and caps.

15 Cut the sterling silver tubing with the saw.

16 Place the cut piece back through the capped bead. Place the capped bead on a steel bench block with one cap down and the other facing up.

17 Use a chasing hammer and riveting tool to gently tap the sterling silver tubing to begin flaring the edge of the tubing. Turn the bead over and repeat the process to flare the opposite side of the tubing.

18 Use the chasing hammer to continue forming the sterling silver tubing into a rivet. Work back and forth on each end until each side is completely flared and the caps are snug. Remember, you are hammering on glass, so use a gentle hand.

Tube-riveted silver bead caps on glass bead by Lisa Blackwell.
Photo by the artist.

Enameling Metal Clay

Glass enameling can be complicated. There are many variables involved when working with glass. This project features Champlevé enameling, which is a design with raised walls of metal clay that surround recessed cells in which the enamel is inlayed. The method of applying the enamel is called "wet packing," which involves filling the cells with wet enamel and then firing the finished clay piece. Because the glass is contained in cells and the piece is relatively small, Champlevé is an easy beginner's enameling project to experiment with. The glass enamel can be fired in an enclosed kiln, but I like to use a unique firing device called the Beehive Kiln, which is perfect for enameling projects. The temperature of the Beehive Kiln stays low enough to soften glass, and due to its open design, you can check the progress of the glass as you work.

MATERIALS YOU'LL NEED FOR ENAMELED
HEART PENDANT:

Art Clay Silver
Basic metal clay tools (see pages 16–18)
Press mold, or rubber stamp
Fine-silver eye pin
Medium temperature, medium expansion,
    lead-free transparent enamel
    powders (see Resources, under
    Thompson Enamel)
Small cup to rinse enamel powders
Distilled water
Dust mask rated for fine particles
Cocktail straw with end cut at an angle
Small pointed scribe
Small round paintbrush, size 0 or 1
Paper towel
Beehive Kiln (see Resources, under JEC
    Products)
Ceramic insert for Beehive Kiln
Tongs for removing ceramic insert
Tile or firebrick for cooling

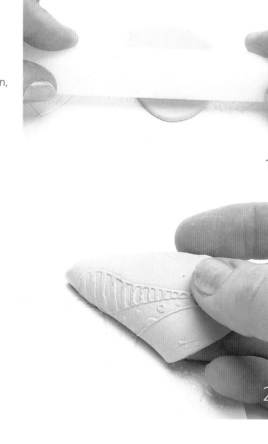

1 Roll out a thick sheet of clay. Press and roll it over a textured mold, or use a rubber stamp to emboss a design into the clay. Remember to oil the mold or rubber stamp to prevent sticking. Use a design such as a line illustration to provide raised edges that will serve as enclosed cells for the glass enamel to fill.

2   Peel the clay from the mold.

3   Trim around the design with a knife, making sure to avoid cutting the raised edge of the design.

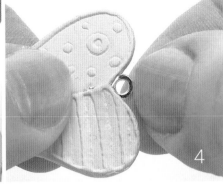

4   Embed a fine-silver eye pin.

5   Let the piece dry. Refine the edges with a file or sanding paper. Fire the piece in a kiln at any of the schedules recommended for Art Clay Silver (see page 37).

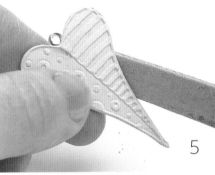

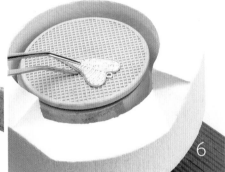

6   After cooling, burnish the piece to bring out the desired shine. Use a burnishing tool to polish the raised edges for a mirror finish. To clean the silver of oils prior to adding the enamel, set it on a ceramic disk and place inside a preheated Beehive Kiln. In this case, the kiln is set on the highest setting. Let the piece heat for two to three minutes with the lid on.

7   Let the piece cool on the disk on a brick or tile after heating. Only handle by the outside edges after cooling; otherwise, you will need to clean again. To prepare the enamels, rinse them to remove the fine dust from the glass. Wear a dust mask that is rated for fine particles when working with enamels, to protect your lungs. Place a small amount of the enamel powder in a cup and rinse a few times with tap water. Swirl the water around gently and then wait for the enamel to settle to the bottom of the cup. Pour off the water, which contains the dust. For the last rinse, rinse with distilled water to keep minerals out of the enamel. The water should be clear when you pour off the last rinse. If not, repeat the process.

8 The enamels will now be ready for wet packing. To lift the enamel grains from the cup, cut the end of a small cocktail straw at an angle and use it as a scoop to spoon the wet glass over your piece. Use the tip of a small paintbrush and a scribe to move the enamel from the straw to the cells to be filled on the silver. The enamel should be like wet sand. If a cell fills with too much water, wick with the corner of a paper towel to gently remove any excess water from the cell as you work.

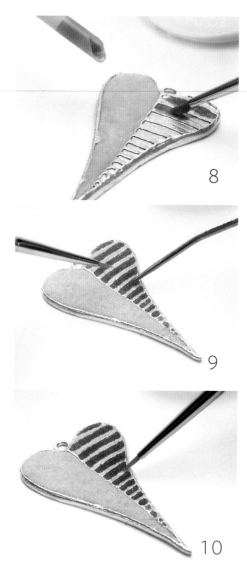

9 Use a scribe in tandem with the paintbrush to pack the cells with an even layer of enamel. The point of the scribe is used to move the grains and to pack them evenly into the cell. This particular design features a shallow relief, and the grains are filled generously to the top of each cell. As the glass flows when heated, the final level of the glass will sit a little lower. If you have deep cells, it is best to work in several layers, heating between each layer rather than making one deep layer of glass.

10 After the cells have been filled with even layers of enamel powder, clean up any stray bits of enamel with a damp, clean paintbrush.

11 Let the piece dry until the water is evaporated from the enamel. To speed drying you can place the piece on a ceramic insert and then place that on top of the Beehive Kiln cover lid as the kiln is heating up.

12 To fire the enamel, place the insert with the clay piece into the preheated kiln. The kiln should be set to the highest setting. Cover with the lid during the firing of the enamel. It should take three to five minutes for the glass to flow.

13 Lift the pan lid to check the progress of the enamel. If it looks bumpy, it is still not ready. This is called the "orange peel" stage, which happens just prior to the glass flowing smooth. The glass moves from a granular state, to an orange peel stage, and then finally to a smooth glossy finish. If you will be adding layers, fire each layer only to the orange peel stage, allowing the last and final layer to progress to the smooth finish. This will prevent over-firing, which can darken the enamel.

14 Leave the clay piece another minute or two and check again. As soon as the glass looks smooth and transparent, it is done.

15 Remove the insert and finished clay piece with tongs and place it on a tile or other heatproof surface to cool. Cool slowly without exposing to cold air or water, as quick cooling will crack the glass.

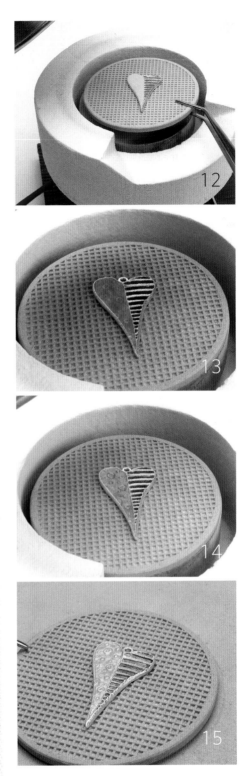

This fine-silver heart pendant enameled with glass was made by Sherri Haab. The heart press mold design was created by Wendy Wallin Malinow, and is available at www.sherrihaab.com.

Glass

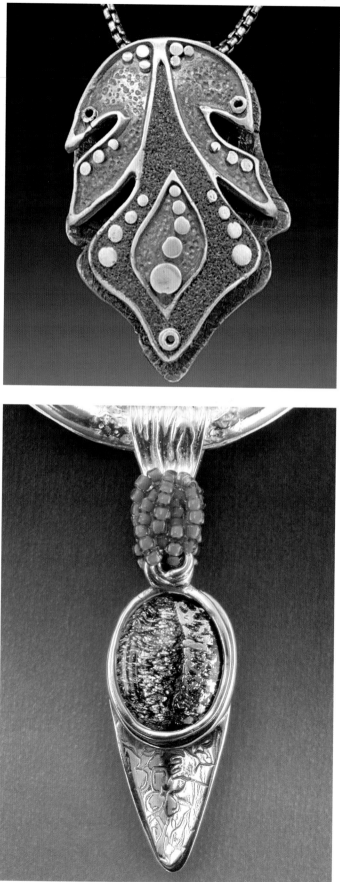

top: *Blue Necklace* by Lynn Glazzard. Focal bead enamel on Art Clay Silver with lampwork glass beads, clasp, and spacer beads. Photo by the artist.

top right: *Enameled Leaf* by Susan Breen Silvy. Photopolymer plate-embossed fine silver metal clay with mixed enamel colors fired to a sugar texture. Stilt riveted to a fine metal clay base. Photo by Jerry Anthony.

bottom right: *Two-Part Pendant* by Donna Penoyer. Fine silver with dichroic glass pendant and seed beads. Photo by the artist.

contributing artists

Lorena Angulo
www.lorenaangulo.com

Emma Baird
www.artclayscotland.com

Lisa Blackwell
www.zoaart.com

Lisa Call
www.lisamariecall.com

Sherry Fotopoulos
www.pmc123.com

Lynne Glazzard
www.lynne-glazzard.co.uk

Michelle Haab
www.littleprints-charming.com

Liz Hall
www.lizardsjewelry.com

Nancy Hamilton
www.bellaluloo.com

Lora Hart
www.lorahart.com

Hadar Jacobson
www.artinsilver.com

Jennifer Kahn
www.jenniferkahnjewelry.com

Christina Leonard
www.christinaleonard.com

Wendy Wallin Malinow
www.wendywallinmalinow.com

Catherine Davies Paetz
www.cdpdesigns.com

Donna Penoyer
www.donnapenoyer.com

Mardel Rein
www.cooltools.us

Jonathan David Sabin
www.jsabin.com

Susan Breen Silvy
www.susansilvy.com

Barbara Becker Simon
www.bbsimon.com

Shahasp Valentine
www.precieux.com

Debra Weld
www.debraweld.com

Catherine Witherell
www.happydayart.typepad.com

resources

PRODUCTS

AMACO®
800-374-1600
www.amaco.com
PolyBlade clay-cutting blades, polymer clay, tools, and cutters

Art Clay World, USA
866-381-0100
www.artclayworld.com
Art Clay Silver products, metal clay supplies, and tools

Clay Factory Inc.
877-728-5739
www.clayfactoryinc.com
Polymer clay, tools, general supplies

Cool Tools
888-478-5060
www.cooltools.us
Metal clays, findings, kilns, gemstones, glass, videos, articles, and tutorials

Creative Catalyst Productions Inc.
www.ccpvideos.com
Metal clay videos

Creative Paperclay®
805-484-6648
www.paperclay.com

Enamelwork Supply Co.
800-596-3257
www.enamelworksupply.com
Glass enamels and supplies

Environmental Technology Inc.
707-443-9323
www.eti-usa.com
Envirotex Lite Epoxy Resin, EasyMold® silicone putty

Fire Mountain Gems
800-355-2137
www.firemountaingems.com
Fine-silver wire, findings, stringing supplies

Hadar Jacobson
www.artinsilver.com
Hadar's Clay™ Metal Clay powder in bronze and copper, books, videos

Harbor Freight
800-444-3353
www.harborfreight.com
Hardware, tools, metal punches, letter stamps

Jacquard Products
800-442-0455
www.jacquardproducts.com
Pearl Ex powdered pigments

JEC Products Inc.
309-523-2600
www.jecproducts.com
Ultra-Lite Beehive Kiln, PMC products,
tools, and accessories

Kemper Tools
909-627-6191
www.kempertools.com
Klay Kutters and other sculpting tools and
supplies

Metal Clay Findings
888-999-6404
www.metalclayfindings.com

Metal Clay Supply
800-388-2001
www.metalclaysupply.com
PMC clay, tools, starter kits, training
DVDs, MultiMandrel™, HattieS products,
BRONZclay and COPPRclay

Metal Clay Tool Kits
609-397-9550
www.pmctoolandsupply.com
Tools, kits, certification classes

Micro-Mark
908-464-2984
www.micromark.com

Plaid Enterprises Inc.
800-842-4197
www.plaidonline.com
Mod Podge® decoupage glue

PMC Connection
866-PMC-CLAY
www.pmcconnection.com
PMC products, tools, jewelry findings,
stones, and kilns

Polyform Products
www.sculpey.com
Sculpey™ and Premo® polymer clay
products

Polymer Clay Express
800-844-0138
www.polymerclayexpress.com
Polymer clay, clay-shaping tools, blades,
clay cutters, findings, and tools

Prairie Craft
800-779-0615
Polymer clay, tools, pattern cutters,
carving tools

Rio Grande
800-545-6566
www.riogrande.com
PMC products and supplies, jewelry
findings, kilns, torches, epoxy resin, and
Cold Mold™ mold-making supplies

Scratch Art
800-377-9003
www.scratchart.com
Shade-Tex® Rubbing Plates

Sherri Haab Designs
www.sherrihaab.com
Books, workshops, craft kits, Image
Transfer Solution™, E3 Etch™

Silpak Inc.
909-625-0056
www.silpak.com
Silputty® RTV

Smooth-On
www.smooth-on.com
Equinox® 35 Fast Silicone Putty, resin,
and casting supplies

Speedball® Art Products
800-898-7224
www.speedballart.com
V-shaped line cutters, Speedy Stamp™
Blocks

Tandy Leather Factory
800-433-3201
www.tandyleather.com
Leather, hardware, tools, and supplies

Thompson Enamel
859-291-3800
www.thompsonenamel.com
Glass enamels, supplies, and tools

Thunderbird Supply Co.
505-722-4323
www.thunderbirdsupply.com

UGotGlass?
866-DICHRO-A
www.ugotglass.com
Dichroic glass, metal clay, findings, and
supplies

Volcano Arts
209-296-6535
www.volcanoarts.biz
Jewelry-making supplies, rivets, metal
blocks, and anvils

Whole Lotta Whimsy
www.wholelottawhimsy.com
PMC, kilns, stones, metal clay, and
enameling supplies

ORGANIZATIONS AND GUILDS

Art Clay Society
www.artclaysociety.com

Metal Clay Academy
www.metalclayacademy.com

PMC Guild
www.pmcguild.com

Index